TALIAFERRO

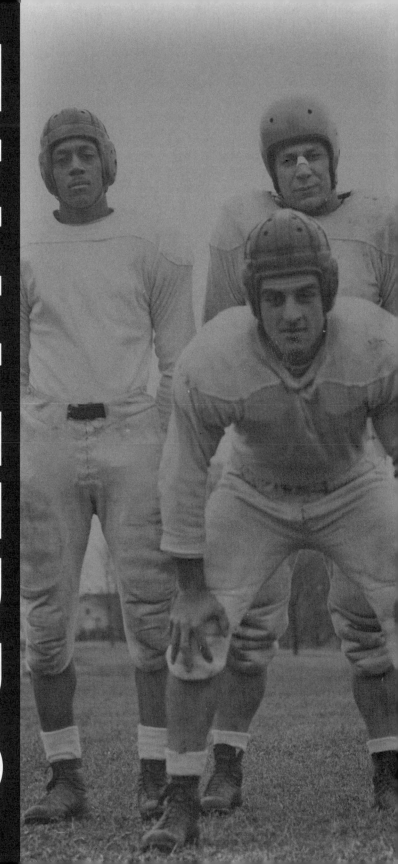

TALIAFERRO

Breaking Barriers from the NFL Draft to the Ivory Tower

Dawn Knight

INDIANA
UNIVERSITY
PRESS

Bloomington • Indianapolis

This book is a publication of

Indiana University Press
601 North Morton Street
Bloomington, IN 47404-3797 USA

http://iupress.indiana.edu

Telephone orders   800-842-6796
Fax orders   812-855-7931
Orders by e-mail   iuporder@indiana.edu

Library of Congress Cataloging-in-Publication Data

Knight, Dawn (Dawn K.)
  Taliaferro : breaking barriers from the NFL draft to the ivory tower /
Dawn Knight.
     p. cm.
  Includes bibliographical references and index.
  ISBN-13: 978-0-253-34931-6 (cloth)
1. Taliaferro, George, 1927- 2. Football players—United States—
Biography. 3. African American football players—Biography.
4. Indiana University, Bloomington—Football—History. 5. Racism in
sports—United States—History—20th century. I. Title.
  GV939.T25K65 2007
  796.332092—dc22
  [B]

                                        2007003268

1 2 3 4 5   12 11 10 09 08 07

To George for inspiring me and
trusting me with your story

To A.J., Taylor, and Mackenzie
with all my love

To Jon for making me
feel special every day;
you have my heart forever

Don't be damned; be somethin' important.
                                    —George Taliaferro

CONTENTS

FOREWORD

I have felt a far-off kinship with George Taliaferro for a long time. While he is my dad's age, we have similar backgrounds. In fact, I feel I have followed in his footsteps in a lot of ways and that the path was much smoother because of him. George was a great football player, but his story is about much more than that. He was one of the first great African American players in the Big Ten and went on to become the first African American to be drafted and the first to play quarterback in the NFL.

That was two generations ago, and some things George Taliaferro had to go through seem unimaginable now. *Taliaferro* chronicles a journey through college and professional football that was uncharted territory in the 1940s. It tells a story of talent, character, and perseverance coming together in a man who helped change the landscape of football, much as Jackie Robinson did for baseball.

If this book were only about football exploits it would be fun to read. But it goes deeper than that. It's a history lesson that gives some insight into how the social structure of Indiana University and the NFL was changed by a very strong-willed person.

I mentioned following in George's footsteps. In 1973 I enrolled at the University of Minnesota, primarily because I wanted to play quarterback. The Big Ten had a strong history of black quarterbacks, and that tradition was started by George Taliaferro. In 2003 I became the first African American head coach of the Indianapolis Colts—fifty years after George had become the Colts's first African American quarterback. Every African American in the NFL today owes a debt of gratitude to George, and I am thrilled that his story is now finally being told.

Tony Dungy
Head Coach
Indianapolis Colts

ACKNOWLEDGMENTS

There are so many people to thank for making this book happen. First, of course, I would like to thank George Taliaferro for telling me his story and for inspiring me with his life. His patience with me on this project is also appreciated; it was shelved a number of times as I was busy starting a family and career. Also to be thanked are my husband, Jon, and my kids: A.J., Taylor, and Mackenzie. Although the book sometimes took a back seat to them, there were also a number of occasions when the opposite was true. They never wavered in their support. Jon also spent hours reading and editing for me. A special thanks goes to NFL coach Tony Dungy, who, like the coaches and players of the '50s era, makes himself accessible to the public even though today it isn't expected. He granted me an interview for this project, and he wrote the foreword. Thank you to Craig Kelley, Indianapolis Colts Public Relations Director, who put me in touch with Coach Dungy and went through Taliaferro's file in the Colts archives with me. My alma mater, Indiana University, provided me with a first-rate education which also afforded me the opportunity to meet George Taliaferro. Indiana University has also continued to help me in this endeavor. The media relations department at the Athletics Office and Brad Cook and the curators at the IU Archives have been especially helpful, along with editors at Indiana University Press: Lee Sandweiss, Linda Oblack, Miki Bird, and Jen Maceyko. Mark Shaw, an author and friend, provided invaluable insight into the publishing process, for which I will be forever grateful. Although the idea for this book began long before I decided to get a master's degree in journalism, Ball State University professors Mark Massé, Beverly Pitts, Ray Begovich, and adviser Dan Waechter were a key part of developing the idea into a final product. Jim Baumgartner at the College Football Hall of Fame has been a source of information and encouragement. Thanks also to Mrs. Viola Taliaferro, who was kind enough to allow me to interview and learn from her. There were interviews with a number of people who know George Taliaferro in some capacity, all of which became important information, whether in the foreground or background. Michelle Haas did some research for me at the Wells Library at Indiana University. Linda Haas, John Hartman, and Ellen Mathia went all over South Bend and Chicago to track down articles about the 1949 draft. The librarians at the South Bend Public Library, Indiana University South Bend Library, and Chicago Public Library were extremely helpful. To all of these people and more: I appreciate the help I received in order to be able to pass on George Taliaferro's story to others.

Trick or Treat

"Thanks, nigger," the little boy said. He didn't say it viciously; he just said it in the same tone as if he were thanking anyone else.

George Taliaferro had opened the door and was greeted with the customary "trick or treat!" Three young trick-or-treaters, a girl about ten and her two younger brothers, who were probably five and seven, stood on his doorstep, their arms extended, holding bags out in anticipation. They were all wearing white; the girl was in some kind of a princess costume. The boys were just wearing white short-sleeved shirts and white pants. October in southern Indiana can be pretty warm, so none of them were wearing jackets. He wasn't sure what the boys were supposed to be. *Maybe they're ghosts,* he thought.

Taliaferro answered the door with one hand while he balanced a large bowl of candy in the other. "Do I get some of yours, or do I give some to you?" Taliaferro had teased when they greeted him with their trick-or-treat chorus. The kids quickly informed him that it was definitely his job to provide the treat. He had laughingly obliged, bending to put a good-sized handful into each bag. As he chuckled, the laugh lines around his eyes multiplied.

"Thank you!" the two oldest had said.

Before he could reply, the third, the youngest, had said, "Thanks, nigger." It sounded like something he said a lot, like saying "ball" or "car" or other words young boys would often pronounce. It flowed as naturally from his mouth as "peanut butter." But it wasn't like that at all, because words like those didn't surprise Taliaferro; they didn't hurt; they were expected from the mouths of young boys.

Maybe I heard it wrong, Taliaferro had told himself. Maybe that wasn't what the boy said after all. Before he could convince himself otherwise, however, the boy's sister had sternly shushed him, confirming what Taliaferro had already known but hadn't wanted to believe. Taliaferro shook his head. It was 2005. Of course racism still existed, still exists. Taliaferro knew that as well as anyone. But it was Halloween; there were kids and costumes and candy. Princesses and pirates were giggling, glowing necklaces guiding their way as their parents pulled their younger siblings in wagons. The word was unexpected, especially from the mouth of a sandy-haired five-year-old on a warm Halloween night in an upper-middle-class neighborhood in Bloomington, Indiana.

Taliaferro had experienced racism in Bloomington before, but significant changes, some inspired by him, had occurred since he had played football for Indiana University in the 1940s and lived in a segregated Bloomington. This neighborhood was also different from the working-class neighborhood he had lived in when he played football for all-black Gary Roosevelt High School in Gary, Indiana. It was in that neighborhood, however, that Taliaferro was first recognized for his football prowess, and it was football that had removed him from the relative shelter from racism that his Gary neighborhood had provided.

Taliaferro's Football Roots

"I want to be a boxer," George Taliaferro told his mother. Young boys often emulate their favorite professional athletes, but in the late 1930s, the only African American professional athletes were boxers and baseball players, and the baseball players could only play in the segregated Negro League. Jackie Robinson hadn't yet shattered the barrier that kept young African American boys from dreaming. Naturally, then, Taliaferro wanted to be a boxer. His mother had heard what he had said and probably would have preferred to ignore him, but she knew that he, as young boys do, would hold on to the idea. Virnater Taliaferro looked at her son, who was already getting bigger than she was, with the knowing look all moms give when they know ahead of time that they've won an argument. "You can be a boxer, but you can't live in this house," she responded matter-of-factly. She had him, and she knew it. Taliaferro quickly determined that leaving the source of "three squares and a flop" could only be bad decision making. So, he turned his sights to the unattainable. He would be a professional football player. But like baseball at the time, there was a pronounced color line in professional football, making Taliaferro's dream unrealistic. Growing up in an integrated neighborhood, however, left him naïve to his situation. Someday, he decided, he was going to play for the Chicago Bears. Luckily, no one told him how unlikely that was.

If he was going to be serious about becoming a football player, he was going to have to get his hands on a football. Taliaferro enlisted the help of his friends, and together they scoured their Gary, Indiana, neighborhood for cans and other items they could sell. Their persistence paid off. They managed to earn enough money to buy a football, a precious commodity. They spent an entire afternoon testing it out, laughing as they played catch, made tackles, and planned strategy. When it was time to go home, they had a tough decision to make: who would get to take the ball along? After discussing it, they decided that the Taliaferro house, which was located on the 2600 block of Madison, was the most centrally located. One of Taliaferro's friends lived on the 2400 block; the other on the 2800 block. Keeping their prized possession at his house would make it easy for each of them to retrieve the ball when they needed it. Not that there would be that many times when they weren't together playing with it anyway.

Football quickly replaced other sandlot games, like Cock the Rooster, a game involving any number of kids who had to remain inside a set of drawn boundaries. One person, the rooster, had to tackle as many people as he could. Anyone who was tackled or who ran out of bounds became a rooster, too. There was no other organization to the game, but Taliaferro partially credits it with the style of running he developed later as a football player. Often winning by avoiding tackles until he was the last one standing, Taliaferro believes it was good preparation for when he would become a halfback. "Just add a ball and some equipment and you have a halfback," he said.

While he and his friends occasionally still played Cock the Rooster, football was more often the game of choice. They named their sandlot team for the street they lived on. The Madison Street Tigers did not limit themselves to football; they also played baseball and basketball at Circus Field against other sandlot teams in their neighborhood. Sometimes Taliaferro would be so excited to get up and play football in the morning that he would get out of bed at 9:30 or 10:00 at night and eagerly ask his mother, "Is it morning yet?" She would shake her head, send him back to bed, and tell him to wait until morning. It was hard to fall asleep on those nights of football dreams.

It is not surprising that these sandlot games were a source of entertainment for Taliaferro and his friends. Their neighborhood was made up of modest one-story homes in the heart of Gary, a steel town located just 30 miles east of Chicago on the shore of Lake Michigan. Gary, Indiana, was actually created by the U.S. Steel Corporation in 1906 for the sole purpose of steel production. It was even named after the corporation's chairman of the board, Elbert H. Gary. Having been developed for the steel industry, the focus was on the mills themselves and not on planning the town, which was thus left largely to land speculators. It didn't take long for slums to develop. The steel mill's workers, made up of a large immigrant population and African Americans, populated the city. The city was defined by the relationships between various ethnic groups and its dependence on the steel industry. This dependence left Gary particularly vulnerable during the Great Depression. The decline of the steel industry continued well into the twentieth century, and by the late 1980s and 1990s, Gary had become a city with one of the highest murder rates in the world, a fact Taliaferro attributed to the loss of the steel mills and the increase in drug use on the streets. This, however, was not the town of George Taliaferro's childhood. Although because of the Depression life could sometimes be financially difficult, the Gary of Taliaferro's youth was a much different place.

Taliaferro was born in Gates, Tennessee, on January 8, 1927, where he lived just down the street from *Roots* author Alex Haley. His family moved when he was just an infant to "the region," as Gary, Indiana, and other northwestern Indiana cities are sometimes referred, probably because of their close proximity to Chicago. Life in Gary, for the Taliaferros and other steel mill families, often meant financial hardship, but it also allowed for unique interaction of different ethnic groups. Despite the economic struggles, Taliaferro said his completely integrated neighborhood was "the way all towns ought to be." It may have been the socioeconomic equality of the people in the neighborhood, or the fact that those who weren't black were immigrants, sharing similar experiences, having come from Italy, Germany, Croatia, Poland, Serbia, and other mainly European countries. They all got along. Pig roasts, a part of the Serbian culture, became a regular part of life for all of the neighborhood families. A Serbian family would slowly roast a pig on a big spit, and the rest of the families would bring side dishes. It didn't matter that the kids were of different races; they were friends. The kids played together without incident while the adults cooked and talked, often about sports and local athletes. "It was a melting pot," Taliaferro said.

Like the Taliaferro home, most homes in the area were modest one-stories. The only exception was the home directly across the street. It was the biggest home in the neighborhood, with two stories and a basement, but unlike most it was shared by two families. The Callaways, who had eight children, resided on the first floor and in the basement of the house. Another family lived on the second floor. Like the other homes in the neighborhood, the Callaway home was well kept. Although the homes were small, a lot of pride went into keeping the lawns neatly trimmed and applying fresh coats of paint when needed. There weren't any apartment buildings in the neighborhood, but there were two grocery stores, the small mom-and-pop stores whose owners were neighbors themselves and knew each of their patrons by name. Most of the homes belonged to two-parent families. The only kid Taliaferro knew who belonged to a single-parent home was his close friend Chester "Chet" Davis. Since everyone looked out for everyone else, Chet still had a lot of adults in his life. As Chet said, "Mrs. Taliaferro used to yell at me all the time." Even the teachers at his school lived in the neighborhood and knew the kids by name.

In his neighborhood the children had to obey all the adults, not just their own parents. Taliaferro explained, "If Mrs. Callaway told me to do something it was done. If not, she would call Mom and Dad and I'd be dead anyway." Chores were another expectation of Gary youth. Taliaferro, who was the second oldest, shared chores with his four siblings: older brother James, and younger siblings Rozell, Claude, and Earnestine. The chores were divided, not equally, but based on their ages and abilities, so Taliaferro and his older brother had the bulk of the work. A strong work ethic, developed throughout his youth, became an important aspect of George Taliaferro's character.

When they weren't doing chores, Gary's youth managed to keep themselves busy and out of trouble with outdoor activities like climbing trees, swimming, and playing sandlot baseball and football games. While the children kept themselves entertained, adults also needed an escape from the financial struggles they faced, especially during the Depression. It is no surprise, then, that Gary residents took a keen interest in high school athletics and their star high school athletes, an inexpensive interest that generated a strong sense of community pride. Having developed his skills in those sandlot games, Taliaferro became one of those stars when he attended all-black Gary Roosevelt High School. While his neighborhood was completely integrated, the schools were not. Taliaferro attended Gary Roosevelt, which was an elementary, junior high, and high school. He had never attended another school.

One of Taliaferro's best friends, Nick Miller, had to be driven to school by his father. Despite living only a couple of blocks from Gary Roosevelt, Nick had to attend the farther-away Emerson High School, due to school placement boundaries. Placement in the area schools was based on geography and ethnicity. The northern district was all-white Emerson High School; all-white Gary Lew Wallace was in the south; the central district was all-black Gary Roosevelt. Between Emerson and Roosevelt was the only integrated school in Gary, Froebel High School. Froebel wasn't integrated without some problems, however. According to Steve Walsh's article in the *Gary Post-Tribune*, when Froebel was integrated in 1945, several hundred white students went on strike, and it was a concert for tolerance, including a performance by Frank Sinatra, that helped ease the tension.

Taliaferro's freshman and sophomore years Gary Roosevelt was permitted to compete against all-white schools in track and field. However, football, a full contact sport, was a different matter. Gary Roosevelt was not permitted to compete against white schools in any contact sports, including, of course, football. This made it difficult for the Roosevelt football team, which often had to endure long road trips in order to compete against other all-black schools. Wendell Phillips and DuSable, all-black high schools in Chicago, were among the closest. Indianapolis's Crispus Attucks High School was a couple of hours away but still closer than Vashon and Sumpter High Schools in St. Louis and Lincoln High School in Evansville, Indiana. One of the longest road trips actually took the Roosevelt football team about 800 miles to Tuskegee, Alabama, for a game.

The difficulty in these long road trips was furthered by World War II. Gas rationing and the fact that there were no buses meant the team had to pile into the cars of coaches and teachers, adults who were painfully aware of the reason they had to travel so far for the games. The teenagers on the football team, excited to be doing what they loved, took little notice of it or of the fact that they dressed in hand-me-down uniforms donated by Northwestern University. Taliaferro's uniform hung from his lean frame. It was so big, in fact, that it was literally taped to his body, a stark contrast to the new, perfectly fitted uniforms worn by players in the area's all-white high schools. Since they didn't play against those teams, they were unaware of the contrast. The Gary Roosevelt players had not known any other world than the sheltered lives they led in their Gary neighborhoods. (This would change during Taliaferro's junior year, when "colored" and parochial schools were admitted to the Indiana High School Athletic Association and black and white schools were permitted to compete against each other.)

Besides, Taliaferro was more focused on the thrill of competing and the recognition it brought than on the segregation that forced his team to travel. He reveled in the attention that came with being one of Roosevelt's elite athletes. His athleticism wasn't limited to football, although that was the sport that would eventually take him somewhere. He was also a swimming champion and a part of Gary's state championship track teams of 1944 and 1945. He even set a record on the pole vault of 12'6", which stood for fifteen years. On top of that, he lettered in football, baseball, basketball, and track all four years of high school, earning 16 letters in all. He was basking in the spotlight, enjoying his status as a star athlete.

Natural athletic ability like that which Taliaferro possessed was recognized in Gary, a town some people considered to have one of the best athletic programs in the nation. His success made him a local celebrity. This was especially true at school. Of this attention Taliaferro said simply, "Everybody

in that school loved me for one reason, because I was George Taliaferro."
One such admirer was Sydney Cummings, who lived across the street and
followed his home-town hero around. A couple of years younger, he would
follow Taliaferro home from school and would offer to carry his shoes just
so he could spend time with him. Cummings didn't realize what a special
honor this was. As if they were his life, Taliaferro shined his football cleats
every day. They really were that important, he would point out later, knowing what opportunities his football career had afforded him.

On school nights, Sydney Cummings would be sent to bed early by his
mother, who wanted him to be well rested for school. She didn't realize that
he couldn't go to sleep, not until he heard Taliaferro coming home. He would
lie in bed, staring at the ceiling and listening for the familiar sound of Taliaferro's whistling. It was so quiet on their street he could hear it from halfway
down the block. "That whistlin' thing is what got me. I just got happy when
I heard it," Cummings said. He would wait until Taliaferro got closer, then
he would go to his window and yell, "Hey, Fat [Taliaferro's high school nick-
name], how you doin'?" Taliaferro would always respond, usually gently reminding Cummings that he should be getting to sleep. Then, and only then,
Cummings could fall asleep. His interest in Taliaferro's football success was
so keen he even decided to become a mascot for the team.

Cummings was just one example of the Gary Roosevelt Panthers' fan
base. To satisfy these hardcore football fans Norman S. Werry, sports editor
for the *Gary-Post Tribune,* wrote weekly updates about the exploits of their
beloved football team. Werry often referred to Taliaferro in these articles.
Even when Gary Roosevelt High School did not win, Werry wrote rave re-
views about Taliaferro's performances. A shutout by Hammond Catholic
Central his senior year was just one example. Werry wrote after that game,
"Central intercepted a Roosevelt pass and then got a completion before the
Panthers could put on the brakes and give Taliaferro a chance to get off one
of several booming punts which were a major factor in keeping the Panthers in the game." In another loss against Horace Mann, Werry described
Taliaferro's contribution to the team. "The Panthers wasted no time getting
their touchdown starting the third quarter when George Taliaferro ran the
kickoff back 35 yards to the Mann 40. . . . Then Taliaferro swung wide at his
right end on a weak side sweep for 12 yards and a first down on the Mann
20," he wrote.

Werry's references were even more glowing, of course, after the many
Gary Roosevelt wins, to which Taliaferro was always a major contributor.
After the Froebel game, for example, Werry wrote: "The Panthers did not

count until the third quarter when George Taliaferro ripped over his right guard from three yards out after gaining 15 yards on a pass from Cornelius Sneed. . . . Taliaferro added the extra point with a perfect placement to complete the scoring in one of the wackiest games ever engaged in by any Steel City rivals." "Ugliest" might have been a better term for the game as there were 14 total fumbles. Still, Taliaferro's impressive performance allowed his team to eke out a 7 to 0 win over Froebel.

Tom Kennedy also wrote about Taliaferro's performances. In another win against South Bend Central, he wrote: "Hard hitting George Taliaferro turned in one of his customary bang-up performances on the turf of Gleason field. . . . Taliaferro put Roosevelt out in front at the outset when he whipped a nifty 21-yard pass to quarterback Charles White. . . . Roosevelt came up with its best drive in the fourth period to account for its final score. It covered 62 yards and ended with Taliaferro going six yards on a center smash to score standing up. On the play previous he had passed 21 yards to Johnny Nickols for a first down."

The last game of the season, against Tolleston, was no exception. Taliaferro contributed with three major punts, including a 64-yarder into the end zone and a 76-yarder. It wasn't just Taliaferro's punts that were impressive that night, however. "[Taliaferro] cut sharply over his left tackle and outran the Raider secondary for a 56-yard touchdown," Werry wrote. With two touchdowns and an extra point Taliaferro had earned the position of third in points in the state, and Gary Roosevelt came off the season with its best record in years at five wins and three losses.

Panther fans, excited about their winning season, showered the team and its stars with attention. While the accolades should have been satisfying for Taliaferro, he found himself frustrated by a system he was just beginning to realize was keeping him from attaining everything he was capable of doing. Sure he was enjoying the recognition his star status brought, and Werry had eloquently praised him all season for his football prowess. He had even managed to draw the attention of some college recruiters. Taliaferro was beginning to see beyond the immediate gratification his ability brought, however, and to recognize the reality of the racism that kept him from achieving his full potential. When recruiters asked if he had won any awards, he could only give a negative reply.

This would have been easier to swallow if his lack of awards had been due to a lack of ability or a lack of motivation on his part. But this simply was not the case; the numbers spoke for themselves. Most frustrating to Taliaferro was that he lacked not the skill, but the skin color to receive these honors.

Because it was an all-black school, Gary's athletes were not eligible for any post-season honors. "We were not recognized because we were black—for no other reason, and this frustrated me," Taliaferro said of the situation.

Taliaferro wasn't the only person who thought he was deserving of an award. Bob Hammel, Indiana's first Mr. Football, wrote an article for the Bloomington *Herald-Times* in 1995. The subject was past football players whom Hammel thought would have been named Mr. Football if that honor had existed when they were playing. Hammel's list included Les Bingaman of Gary Lew Wallace (who went on to be an all-pro center for the Detroit Lions) and George Taliaferro. Taliaferro was flattered by Hammel's recognition; however, he also felt compelled to let him know the truth. He would not have been considered for the honor even if it had existed, he explained, because the color of his skin would have made him ineligible.

In a time of blatant segregation, it was Taliaferro's football prowess that was going to create opportunities for him, though he was unaware of that at the time. His unique ability to run, pass, and kick, and do it all well, made him a triple threat on the football field. Often he would score the touchdown and then follow it by earning the extra point. This, he said, was what made him such a valuable player: "They [opponents] never knew what I was going to do with the ball, and I could do anything that needed to be done. I could throw it. I could kick it. I could catch it. I could run with it. And the defenses that were set up specifically to stop me were not what they would have set up for anybody else. They could not take risks when the ball came to me. So what they had to do was to spread out and keep me from darting through the holes," he explained.

Not only was Taliaferro a triple threat on offense, but he was equally as skilled on defense. This, and a little luck, started him on the road to trailblazing. His most notable game of the season finally earned him some real attention outside of Gary, attention that also led to a football scholarship. Ironically, it was a game Gary Roosevelt was never anticipated to play. This game, which was never on the schedule, went against the status quo because it pitted all-black Gary Roosevelt against an all-white school. This game against football powerhouse East Chicago Roosevelt, the product of a fluke chance, changed the course of George Taliaferro's life.

East Chicago was not the average high school football team. It was quite the opposite, in fact. In the early 1940s "East Chicago Roosevelt was," according to an article by sportswriter Mike Whicker, "the Goliath of Indiana high school football." The undefeated Rough Riders "owned the gridiron. [They were] the colossus no one could beat." He advised their potential opponents:

"Don't even try. Just take your lumps and be thankful you walked away." Gary Roosevelt, it seemed, would be attempting to do the impossible.

Having an open date at the end of its schedule was not the kind of preparation East Chicago's coach Pete Rucinski wanted for his championship-bound team. He worried that not playing for two weeks would soften his players. He wanted them to remain sharp and focused, so he needed to schedule a game that would challenge his team and keep them geared up for the championship game. In Gary Roosevelt High School he saw the perfect solution. Gary Roosevelt would be available to play an unscheduled game. However, it was also a first-rate team that would provide sufficient challenge to his players. Pete Rucinski contacted Gary Roosevelt's coach, Bo Mallard, and explained his desire to have the two teams meet. Mallard agreed to the scrimmage, and they set the date. Neither coach realized at the time the impact their conversation would have. It set into motion events that not only would change the course of one young man's life, but ultimately would impact a system of segregation and the sport of football as a whole.

Rucinski and Mallard scheduled the game, and the Gary Roosevelt Panthers were geared up and ready to play. The game afforded them the opportunity to compete against a school that had previously been off limits to them as an opponent; it was their chance to prove themselves. They understood what a football power they were facing, but they did not let it discourage them. Taliaferro was up for the challenge, but he couldn't help but be nervous. He knew they were playing against a notorious East Chicago football team that would provide more competition than he and his teammates had ever faced. This time they did not have to take a long road trip to get there; the game was practically in their own back yard. There would be a lot of people he knew, probably his entire neighborhood, watching this game.

Before the game, Coach Mallard launched into his usual locker-room pep talk. He wanted to get his team mentally prepared for the challenge they were about to face. "Football is a team sport," he told them, "but each member has to fight an individual battle as well. If one person makes a good block, then another one can score." He continued by stressing the importance of the fundamentals, blocking and tackling. When Coach Mallard finished his pep talk, his Panthers ran onto the field to face the heavily favored East Chicago Rough Riders, a team, Whicker wrote, that was "devouring their foes like some hungry behemoth."

No one, including the players, was surprised when East Chicago took an early lead. Their first score came on a 50-yard drive, and it didn't take long for them to add two points to their lead with a safety, when the Panthers had trouble fielding the kickoff. At the end of the first quarter, the Panthers found themselves already trailing the Rough Riders by nine points. Getting behind early to East Chicago meant an uphill battle for Gary Roosevelt. They managed to keep their hearts and heads in the game despite the fact that many of the spectators had already counted them out. Their steely resolve paid off about halfway through the second quarter when Leroy Allen scored on a 50-yard drive, as *Gary Post-Tribune* sportswriter Joe Kutch wrote, through "the entire East Chicago defense."

The Panthers heeded Mallard's locker-room advice and focused on basic blocking and tackling, somehow managing to keep the Rough Riders from scoring the rest of the game. There were some "lumps" involved in this defensive battle. According to Kutch, "Play had to be stopped on several occasions to revive some of the boys who got hit a little too hard." Roosevelt's offense managed to sneak in a touchdown, making the score 7 to 9. Then Gary Roosevelt got possession of the ball with an opportunity not only to close the gap, but also to take the lead from their new rivals. This is when, "taking advantage of the edge which the versatile Taliaferro gained with his booming punts, the Gary gridders found themselves on the Twin City men's twenty-two yard line," Kutch wrote. Coach Mallard managed to pull one over on East Chicago's Coach Rucinski the final play of the game. Cornelius Sneed, the quarterback, threw the ball to Taliaferro, who usually played tailback. Kutch described what happened next: "Taliaferro snagged the ball on the two-yard line and then argued with a host of Rider tacklers before ending up on the seat of his pants with the upset victory in the bag."

In Indiana high school football history, East Chicago Roosevelt High School is in the record books for winning 34 straight games from 1944 through 1948. The game against Gary Roosevelt's Panthers, an unscheduled game against an unlikely rival, did not count. To Taliaferro, however, this mattered very little. To him the satisfaction of beating the state's powerhouse was still an overwhelming feeling, even if his team wouldn't get formal recognition for it. "A fighting Gary Roosevelt football team which wouldn't believe what everybody was saying about that powerful East Chicago Roosevelt eleven went out to the lair of the Rough Riders last night and didn't start home until they had licked the previously unbeaten boys 13 to 9," Kutch wrote. He had to preface the article title with a statement about his honesty, just in case anyone doubted him. The article, "No Foolin', Panthers Trip Rough Riders, 13-9" came out the next day.

The title is not surprising given the fact that even Gary Roosevelt's football players couldn't believe they had won. "It was hard to imagine that Gary

Roosevelt had beaten East Chicago Roosevelt," Taliaferro said of his and his teammates' initial reaction. Although it was the most important game he had ever played, his parents were not there to see his game-winning moment. This was nothing new; they never saw a single game of their college-bound son's high school football career. It wasn't that they didn't care; they just didn't understand the game, Taliaferro said.

Virnater Taliaferro was a heavyset woman with a sixth-grade education. She had almost kept her son from playing football. It was a dangerous sport, she had decided, and one she did not want to see her son playing. When he had first brought home a permission slip for her to sign so he could play, she had refused to do so. It wasn't like the sandlot games he and his friends had played. They were just kids then and there were no pads involved. She didn't like the idea of him playing on the school team, which she felt would be more dangerous. Taliaferro, who was determined to play, wouldn't accept no for an answer. He continued to press her until she finally agreed to sign, but only under certain conditions. First, she said, he had to submit to a physical exam, one that she, the family "doctor," would give Taliaferro herself. It was an exam, Taliaferro says, "few human beings and no animals could pass" and it was a ritual for the four years he was in high school. The other condition was that Taliaferro had to get a copy of the rules and requirements for the football team from Coach Mallard.

Having satisfied all of her conditions, Taliaferro was finally given her permission to play for Gary Roosevelt's football team. He took a lot of pride in this and every night he came home from practice with his jock straps, underwear, and socks for her to launder. Then he would sit down and shine his football shoes. Football had become his life, and it showed. He was tearing up the field every game. In a 1993 article by Al Hamnik, Taliaferro's Roosevelt teammate J. Donald Leek described him: "He could really take care of business. He'd run by you, over you, whatever was required. George [Taliaferro] played every game, every down. We didn't platoon in those days. You played until the game was over or you got hurt, whichever came first." The East Chicago game was no exception.

Taliaferro's performance and game-winning touchdown had not disappointed his loyal Gary fan base. Werry, as usual, reported on the game. "This one goes into the book as one of the all-time upsets in Calumet schoolboy football," he wrote. Taliaferro, who was still having a hard time believing they had won, kept playing it over and over in his head. He remembered cradling the ball, dropping on his butt in the end zone, and holding onto the ball, "as if it were life itself." In an interesting twist of fate, it was. Because it was his performance during this game that would change the course of Taliaferro's life forever. Taliaferro, though not yet famous for his "triple threat" abilities, had played the game of his life. Kutch wrote: "Leading the Panther gridders was [George] Taliaferro, a young man who can do anything a star should be able to do. His bone-crushing tackles, powerful running and long-distance booting would make any coach smile with satisfaction." Any coach but the one on the other team, that is. Taliaferro's performance had not gone unnoticed by East Chicago coach Pete Rucinski.

"Rucinski became my greatest admirer," Taliaferro said. Rucinski had even joked that his team would never play Gary Roosevelt again. But Rucinski was altogether serious when he contacted a personal friend, Indiana University football coach Bo McMillin to tell him of his discovery. Rucinski described Taliaferro's triple-threat performance against his own previously undefeated Rough Riders. He told McMillin he should seriously consider recruiting George Taliaferro. Rucinski had, Taliaferro said, convinced McMillin that there was no better tailback in the state of Indiana. Rucinski's advice did not fall on deaf ears.

In fact, Bo McMillin wasted no time in dispatching J. C. "Rooster" Coffee to Gary to talk to Taliaferro and Coach Bo Mallard. The trio met in Mallard's office. Coffee, a guard, was one of just a handful of black players on Indiana University's football team. As a student at Indiana University (IU), Coffee had also helped President Herman B Wells integrate the gymnasium's pool. According to Bob Cook, a former Indiana University athletic director and McMillin biographer, Wells had asked for the most popular black athlete and was told about Coffee. According to Taliaferro, Wells urged Coffee to just: "Go in [the pool] and don't ask anybody." Coffee obliged Wells by jumping into the whites-only pool.

Coffee's personality was probably one of the reasons he was such a popular athlete and why it was simply accepted when he jumped into the university's whites-only swimming pool—in the nude. Strangely, health code regulations at the time required nudity in the pool. While Coffee was not the first black man to jump into the pool, he was the first to do it and get away with it. According to Taliaferro, another black man, J. B. Clark jumped into the pool once, but was immediately kicked out. Subsequently, the pool was drained of its water to be replaced by fresh, new water, presumably that had not touched the skin of a black man. It was an altogether different story when Coffee, the popular athlete, jumped in. No one complained, other black students also began to use the pool, and soon it was integrated without incident.

Coffee's status as an athlete and his dynamic personality probably had a lot to do with the pool's successful integration. In the McMillin biography, Cook wrote of a time when McMillin was having the team work on a new offensive maneuver and was becoming frustrated with the lack of progress. McMillin had said, "Daggone it. This play could be a topper, and we're going to work on it until we're black in the face." According to Cook, Coffee responded, "Well, Coach, I guess that means I can go in." Everyone had a good chuckle. Coffee, then, was an ideal candidate to visit Taliaferro, who could relate to another popular black athlete.

Despite having Coffee help recruit Taliaferro, there was doubt whether he would actually play for the Indiana University Hoosiers. There were a lot of forces working against such an outcome. One obstacle was Taliaferro's Gary fans. Some people from his predominantly African American community were vocal in their reservations about him attending Indiana University. They were suspicious, Taliaferro said, because Coach McMillin hailed from Texas, a place they associated with intense racism. Moreover, Pat McPherson, another popular black athlete who had attended Gary Froebel, had attended IU in the 1930s, only to transfer to all-black Wilberforce in Ohio because of the extreme racism he apparently had faced in Bloomington, Indiana. Gary fans did not want Taliaferro to experience a similar fate. Indiana University, they felt, was just not the right place for their star athlete.

Racism wasn't a big concern for Taliaferro. He had lived most of his life in this Gary neighborhood, where he had been relatively sheltered from the harsh reality of racial discrimination and intolerance. The only advice about racism his parents had ever given him was to just behave himself. They advised him not to give anyone a reason to harm him in the first place. They added that he should live to his potential and never wish ill will toward anyone. This, they told him, would allow him to accomplish his goals.

Gary residents were not the only obstacle coming between George Taliaferro and Indiana University. Other schools, like UCLA and Illinois were also actively recruiting him. In addition, Taliaferro was giving serious consideration to attending North Carolina Central, an all-black college. Naturally, the transition from an all-black high school to an all-black college was an obvious choice. Like so many high school seniors, he had a difficult decision to make. Unlike today's high school seniors, however, racism and World War II played a major role in his decision-making process.

Although World War II was coming to an end, the draft still existed. Mrs. Parham, the Taliaferros' next-door neighbor, was on the draft board. She informed the Taliaferros that their son would have a better chance of being deferred from the draft if he remained in Indiana to attend college. In other words, if he attended Indiana University he would be less likely to be drafted than if he attended one of the other schools he was considering. Of course, the Taliaferros preferred not to have their son fight in the war and encouraged him to take Mrs. Parham's information into serious consideration as he made his decision. So, it was Mrs. Parham who became IU's best recruiter, sealing the deal for Bo McMillin.

Another Gary resident, Ora Wildermuth, would have played a key role in Taliaferro's decision if Taliaferro had been aware of his feelings on integration. Wildermuth was on IU's Board of Trustees, where he was very vocal about his opposition to integration. Taliaferro's neighbor, William Downs, was a domestic worker for Wildermuth. When he was trying to make a decision regarding his college education, Taliaferro considered the fact that Downs had told him Wildermuth was quite fond of Taliaferro. He was unaware that the powerful Indiana alumnus and Board of Trustees member was fighting to keep integration from happening at Indiana University. Tom Graham and his daughter, Rachel Graham Cody, wrote a book about Bill Garrett, the first black basketball player in the Big Ten. In it, they describe Garrett's experiences at Indiana University and Wildermuth's fight to keep segregation. They quote a letter from Wildermuth to the board's treasurer: "I am and shall always remain absolutely and utterly opposed to social intermingling of the colored race with the white." Wildermuth went on to write: "If a person has as much as 1/16th colored blood in him, even though the other 15/16ths may be pure white, yet he is colored." Had Taliaferro known Wildermuth's opposition to integrating Indiana University, he would have risked World War II and the draft (against Mrs. Parham's advice) and attended another school. Today, Indiana University's HPER (Health, Physical Education, and Recreation) building is named in honor of Ora Wildermuth, but most of the students who pass through its doors probably know little about the man it was named after.

Once Taliaferro had decided to attend Indiana, word spread quickly throughout his school. Apparently this drew the concern of some of the educators at Gary Roosevelt who worried that he would be more focused on football than on academics at IU. His principal, Mr. H. Theodore Tatum, football coach Bo Mallard, and track coach Leonard Douglas decided to ensure this did not happen. They went to Indiana University to meet with President Herman B Wells. There they impressed upon him the fact that they wanted Taliaferro to earn a college degree and that he was not to be "given" anything, no matter how important he was to the football team. Had the men known Wells and McMillin, they would have understood such a visit was unnecessary.

That doesn't mean their trip was unwarranted. In fact, it was probably brought about by Taliaferro himself, who had some academic problems earlier in his high school career. In fact, he had almost dropped out of school. It was a spontaneous thing; he simply stayed home from school one day and told his parents he planned to quit, that he was wasting time at school when he could be out earning money. He wanted to work in the steel mill like so many other men in Gary, to bring home a paycheck, to be a man. A pact had been made between the U.S. Steel Corporation and the U.S. government that during the war, because so many eligible workers were gone, high school seniors could work at the mill on weekends, even if they were not 18. Taliaferro worked there on weekends his senior year even though he was only 17. He worked in the tin mill, where his father worked. He wanted to quit school to work there full time and help his family, but his father saw things differently.

"No way. Where are you going to live?" Robert Taliaferro asked. "There is no room for two men in this house, and *I* am the man in *this* house," he told his son. "You can take nothing with you. A man can provide for himself," he continued. Those few abrupt words had a big impact on Taliaferro, who wasn't ready to be that independent. His idea had been to earn a paycheck like a man, but to continue to live at home where his meals would be cooked for him, so he was easily convinced to remain in school. While that resolved the issue with his father, however, there was still the issue to be resolved at school.

As he was accustomed to receiving praise following a football game and assumed it was more of the same when Coach Mallard called him to his office, Taliaferro quickly made his way there after class one day. This particular day, however, Mallard wasn't ready to praise. Instead, he looked Taliaferro square in the eyes and said, "Son, you will not be playing football if you do not get your grades up." Forgetting another lesson his father had taught him, Taliaferro lied and said, "Nobody told me that." The conversation with Mallard, however, shocked Taliaferro even more than his father's threat to kick him out. He knew without a doubt he could not give up football. That simply was not an option. He had been living for the sport ever since he and his friends had worked so hard to earn the money to buy that first football. Those sandlot games had created a passion in him. Taliaferro knew he would have to start devoting more time to his studies. It was this that prompted his principal and coaches to visit President Wells. Taliaferro, despite having been taught at an early age to value education, had not always been a model student, and college was going to require even more self discipline, especially with the number of hours that would be devoted to football. His mentors simply wanted to ensure that he would achieve the same success academically as they were already confident he would attain in football.

So, despite a number of obstacles, Taliaferro's decision to play for Indiana University was finally made official, the news quickly spreading throughout his Gary neighborhood. He was the first person in his family to go to college, giving him the opportunity to get the education his parents wanted for him. It wasn't long before he was contacted by *Gary Post-Tribune* editor Norman S. Werry, the man who had so eloquently written about his football accomplishments all season. Werry wanted an interview with the IU-bound football player, and Taliaferro agreed. Still conscious of his role as the local hero, Taliaferro dressed carefully for the interview. He decided on his black and gold Gary Roosevelt letterman "R" sweater which showed off the 16 letters he had earned. He wore it with black pants, so everyone would know that he was still "a dyed-in-the-wool Gary Roosevelt Panther." He was not nervous and, other than his attire, did nothing to prepare for the interview because, as he said, "The only thing I knew without a shadow of a doubt was that I was a good football player and given the chance, I could play with anyone." He had always been confident about his football ability.

His ability, however, would not be the sole focus of the interview. He showed up at the appointed time and after the typical introductions, handshake, and small talk, the interview got underway. Taliaferro explained he had decided to attend IU in the fall where he would, of course, be a member of the Hurryin' Hoosiers football team under Coach Bo McMillin.

"How do you think you are going to make out at Indiana University?" Werry asked him during the interview.

Taliaferro, sitting directly across from him, legs crossed, nonchalantly, and with a hint of the cockiness of a star football player, replied simply, "I should make out okay." He meant it, though. It wasn't bravado; he just knew he could play the game. Werry wasn't looking for that response. He restated the question to clarify.

"I mean, how do you think you are going to adjust to playing with white players?" he asked.

Taliaferro, who had never considered his color a factor in his ability to play football, was taken aback at first. It wasn't that Werry was racist; he was simply asking the question on everyone's mind, including everyone in Taliaferro's neighborhood. There were only a handful of black players at major universities. Racism was sure to come into play. It was the question on the minds of those who had discouraged him from attending Indiana in the first place. How would he make out on Bloomington's segregated campus? Once he was over the initial surprise the question produced in him, Taliaferro managed to answer it. His answer was an early indicator of the combination of confidence, humor, and positive attitude with which he handled obstacles in his football career and in his life. It was this attitude that would ultimately lead to his success. "If they put their pants on one leg at a time, I'll do fine," he answered.

Adjusting to Life at Indiana University

The drive from Gary to Bloomington is a scenic one. Just outside of Gary are miles of flat land, the occasional white farm house scattered amidst the countless corn and soybean fields so often associated with Indiana. As soon as Taliaferro was south of Indianapolis, however, the scenery abruptly changed, much as his life would. He was in the middle of southern Indiana's rolling hills. In the fall people come from all over to see the vibrant autumn shades and the covered bridges tucked away in this hilly landscape. And it is Indiana, so there are basketball hoops on century-old barns.

"This bus driver doesn't even know where Bloomington is," Taliaferro thought as he looked out the window at altogether unfamiliar scenery. In high school he had played a game in Bloomington, but didn't realize that game had been in Illinois and not Indiana. "That's how naïve I was," he said. He was sure the route the Greyhound driver was taking now was not the same one, but everyone else seemed content, so he decided to just keep quiet, even though he suspected they were going the wrong way. Even so, he couldn't stop looking out the windows. He was taking everything in, not wanting to miss a thing, especially when they got to those hills. He had come to Indiana University in April on a recruiting trip, but he was with other athletes and coaches, it was a rainy day, and he didn't pay as much attention to the scenery. This time, he couldn't take his eyes from the changing landscape. Everything was so different than what he was used to. Taliaferro was also thinking about the football season ahead. He had no idea of the many changes that were in store for him upon his arrival.

The self-assurance he had displayed in his recent interview was shaken when Taliaferro arrived in Bloomington in June of 1945. The Greyhound bus finally came to a stop at 10th and Walnut. He happily stretched his lean frame when he got off the bus. Then he collected his things and got a taxi, not realizing that the home where he would be staying was just four blocks away at 8th and Dunn.

Taliaferro had graduated from Gary Roosevelt just a week earlier, on June 14, and by June 21 he had made his way to Bloomington. He came to the university early on an invitation from Coach McMillin, who asked his freshman football players to arrive on campus early in the summer to help make the transition from high school to college a little easier. The players could learn, prior to the start of classes, the location on Indiana University's sprawling campus of classroom buildings, practice fields, and dining areas in order to calculate how long it would take to get from place to place. When football season started, then, they could be more focused. The transition to college life, however, would prove even more difficult for McMillin's black players who had more adjustments to make than merely finding certain locations. For them, it was not just a change in scenery. They also had to adjust to life on a segregated campus, to the invisible line that ran like a thick, ugly wall through Bloomington, cutting it in half, making much of it inaccessible to IU's black students. Taliaferro quickly discovered that he was in unfamiliar territory.

Soon after he arrived on campus, he reported to the football stadium, where he was ushered into a line of freshman players picking up football gear. To his surprise, he was the shortest and lightest person in the line of would-be players. Standing 5'11" and weighing 195 pounds, he found himself in line in front of Pat Kane, who stood 6'3" and weighed 210 pounds, and Tom Schwartz, a 6'5", 215-pounder. Directly in front of Taliaferro was future football team captain John Goldsberry, who was 6'1" and weighed 230 pounds. Their size difference, while apparent to everyone, seemed magnified to Taliaferro. Suddenly he wasn't the confident athlete he had been as one of Gary Roosevelt's stars. He couldn't even fake self-assurance.

He turned to Coach McMillin and asked, "Are they all the same age as me?"

McMillin nodded his head in response.

"I have never seen people this big," Taliaferro said aloud, though more to himself than to his coach. For the first time he began to doubt himself. He couldn't stop the thoughts in his head. *Should I really be here?* He wondered. *They are taller and bigger than any football players I know. Will I fit in here?* He finally had to voice his doubts aloud. It was the only way to get them out of his head. For the first time he wasn't the picture of cool confidence. He finally pronounced, "I am in the wrong place." The question Werry had asked now plagued him. *They were right,* Taliaferro thought, reminding himself of

Indiana University Football coach Alvin Nugent "Bo" McMillin works with his Hurryin' Hoosiers during football practice in July 1945. *Photo courtesy IU Archives.*

the Gary fans who had doubted his decision to attend, who had vocalized doubts the moment they heard Indiana was recruiting him.

This was to be the first of many times Coach Bo McMillin would reassure Taliaferro, both on and off the football field. He had been thoroughly scouted, he assured the shaken Taliaferro. There *is* a place for you on Indiana University's football team, he told him. It wasn't just a statement made to appease him. Taliaferro could hear the sincerity as McMillin went on to explain that he looked forward to the role Taliaferro would play on his football team, that there was a reason he had sent Rooster Coffee to recruit him. McMillin knew football, had actively pursued bringing Taliaferro to Indiana, and knew he should be there, he told Taliaferro. McMillin was right. Taliaferro proved this during his first practice with Indiana while running one of McMillin's favorite plays.

Coach McMillin utilizes a chalk board in the old trophy room of the men's gym to plan strategy. He was always working on ways to trick his opponents, like with his Cockeyed T. Circa 1945. *Photo courtesy of IU Archive*

The "T" formation is just what it sounds like, a football formation that lines the players up in the shape of a "T." At the bottom of the "T" is the quarterback, and there are three running backs placed on the top of the "T": one on each end and one in the middle. This formation, Taliaferro said, had revolutionized football. It featured the use of a forward pass and put enormous pressure on the defense by spreading the offense's ability to use the entire field in a short amount of time. It also, he said, made the game more enjoyable to the fans, who could more easily follow the ball and who saw more scoring with the "T" formation.

Seemingly never satisfied with the ordinary, Coach McMillin, who also loved trick plays, took the "T" formation one step further. Once everyone was using the "T," McMillin had to do something to make it interesting again. Instead of placing one running back on each end and one in the middle, McMillin would run a different version, his own "Cockeyed T." For the Cockeyed T he would not space the running backs evenly. Instead, he would use an unbalanced line and shift the quarterback right behind the guard and the right halfback to the outside end. The fullback was spotted behind the quarterback and the left halfback was four yards behind the center. It seemed to work. "McMillin's Cockeyed T just baffled defenses," Taliaferro said.

McMillin decided to see just what Taliaferro could do. Taliaferro, who lined up as a tailback, handled the ball like a quarterback in the Cockeyed T. The ball was snapped to him, and he could pass, hand it off, or run with it, depending on the play. The first time Taliaferro ran a play in the Cockeyed T during practice, he ran 80 yards for a touchdown. Thinking it was just a fluke, McMillin called for the same play again. Taliaferro again ran 80 yards for a touchdown.

After watching him execute two successive 80-yard runs, McMillin said, "Turn a little to the right, George."

"But Coach, how was it for distance?" Taliaferro replied laughing. His execution of the play was, needless to say, a pleasant surprise for McMillin and promptly became his favorite play for him. "Let George do it," McMillin would yell when he called for it. Taliaferro had earned, despite his comparatively small stature, a starting position for the Indiana Hurryin' Hoosiers, the Cream and Crimson.

While McMillin had encouraged Taliaferro on the field, he made a lasting impression on him in other ways as well. Coach McMillin's character affected Taliaferro, who noticed that his coach, among other things, refused to "arrange" class attendance like other coaches were rumored to do. "My coach believed in winning, but never at all costs," Taliaferro said. McMillin's positive attitude also kept his players grounded. He pushed them on the football field, but he also pushed them to get an education. In fact, McMillin pushed Taliaferro harder in school than his own mother and father, his parents who said to him every day, "We love you. You must be educated," because they knew education was the way he would avoid a long life of working in the steel mills. Taliaferro wondered if this was because McMillin himself had left school without getting a degree, though going back to finish it later. Or perhaps McMillin did not want people to perceive Taliaferro as just some "black dumb jock." Whatever his reason, the coach profoundly affected Taliaferro. "Bo McMillin changed my life," Taliaferro stated of the impact their relationship ultimately had on him.

There were many facets to Alvin "Bo" McMillin, a man who, biographer Bob Cook wrote, did not know his own age and had no birth certificate. The

Coach McMillin on January 15, 1945. McMillin, who hailed from Texas, was sometimes able to move his players to tears with his locker-room talks. *Photo courtesy IU Archives.*

175-pound McMillin was a fairly small man, in his forties, with a full head of grey hair. He had a button nose, big ears, and a Texan drawl. His childhood in Texas had been a struggle. His was a life of poverty, and he had to work hard at a young age to help his family. It may have been this childhood that forged in him a strong desire to champion the underdog. Because "[the underdog's] got something to fight for," McMillin said. This was even the case when he was a college football player himself. As quarterback for Centre College in Danville, Kentucky, Bo McMillin was legendary. In 1921 his 30-yard touchdown run was the only score of the game against a Harvard team that had been unbeaten for five years. The win by the Centre College Prayin' Colonels over Harvard is still considered one of the greatest upsets in college football. McMillin's sole touchdown earned him a ride on his team's shoulders. To sweeten the victory, McMillin, who didn't smoke or drink, but who was known to gamble (the rumor was that it was to help pay his college tuition), had even placed a winning bet on the upset. According to an article by Valarie Ziegler, his touchdown was the most famous one in Centre College football history, and during his entire five-year career at Centre, the team was only beaten three times.

His fame continued as a college football coach when he brought success to other underdogs. He had managed to bring winning seasons to Centenary College in Louisiana, Geneva College in Pennsylvania, and Kansas State University. A 14-year stint at Indiana University before moving onto professional football would be no different. His first four seasons at Indiana also brought the first winning seasons the Hoosiers had seen in years. With success, McMillin also brought humor. Cook wrote that when the coach came to Indiana, knowing the state's fascination with basketball, he had said: "Oh, I love basketball, too. I played it in high school. And I coached it. Like Bob Zuppke [the Illinois coach] always said, 'It's a great recreational sport and something to do between the end of football and the beginning of spring practice.'" McMillin, Taliaferro said, could play any sport, including golf, pool, and even ping pong. McMillin rarely cussed, Taliaferro recalled, but the players could tell he was really upset when he would say, "Go piss in the lake!"

Each year his ability to keep the Old Oaken Bucket at Indiana University earned McMillin more respect from Hoosier fans. The Oaken Bucket game was created out of the high-spirited rivalry between two major Indiana universities, Indiana and Purdue. The two teams had been playing each other for more than 30 years, since 1891, when in 1925 a joint committee of the two schools decided to further the rivalry and excitement of the annual game. In order to do so, they decided that there should be a traditional trophy to go to the winner of the annual match between the two rival football teams. The committee selected a well bucket as the trophy because it was something typically Hoosier, something everyone could associate with Indiana. Each year, possession of the wooden well bucket would go to the winner of the match. A link of either a block letter "I" or block letter "P" to represent the winning school would be attached to the trophy. The block letter links would easily enable the schools and their respective fans to determine who had the bucket in their possession most often, another way to sweeten the victory and intensify the rivalry. The first Oaken Bucket game was played at the dedication of the original Memorial Stadium on Indiana University's campus in Bloomington. It ended in a 0 to 0 tie. Until McMillin came along, Purdue had managed to add more block letters than IU. The Hoosiers, however, began to catch up with McMillin at the helm. The "po' l'il boys," as McMillin called his team, earned more I's for the bucket than Purdue did P's under McMillin's tutelage. It was even rumored that his contract was ripped up after each Oaken Bucket game win and a new contract written offering him more money. In jest, McMillin even began referring to the Old Oaken Bucket as his "meal ticket," according to Cook.

The football field was not the only place McMillin was aggressive. He was

Bo McMillin counts the I's on the Old Oaken Bucket on May 23, 1946.
Under his tutelage, more I's than P's were added to the trophy, a symbol
of the heated rivalry between Indiana University and Purdue University.
McMillin jokingly referred to the bucket as his "meal ticket" because
of rumors that his contract was rewritten after each Oaken Bucket win.
Photo courtesy IU Archives.

also ahead of his time when it came to civil rights. At a time when Big Ten
basketball had a so-called "gentleman's agreement" not to recruit black players, and while some other Big Ten football teams were without black players
altogether, McMillin was not afraid to assert his beliefs. It was not just black
players he was willing to defend, but anyone McMillin saw treated unfairly,
people he saw as underdogs. In the McMillin biography, Cook recounts one
incident involving Indiana's head trainer, Dwayne "Spike" Dixon, who had

a noticeable limp. Dixon's first time on the football field during a game later brought complaints from a fan who called McMillin to voice his opinion about having a "crippled" trainer. Cook wrote that the assistant coaches took the phone away from McMillin after he yelled into the phone, "You object to what? His limp? I hadn't noticed it, does he limp? Look asshole, that limp is a result of a bout with Polio."

And even when most schools, like Purdue and Notre Dame, did not have black players on the roster, "Bo . . . sought them just as actively as he did other prospects," Cook wrote. His pursuit of George Taliaferro was just one example. Cook also recounted an incident at an away game in Kentucky, in which McMillin changed the team's hotel because his black players were not permitted to stay there. This was often the case when teams from the north played teams in the south. Most of the time, the team ended up staying in two different hotels, one for the black players and one for the other members of the team, or the black players would stay in private residences. McMillin wasn't like most coaches, though. When he was told his black players couldn't stay in the hotel, he responded, "Then forget them. Find a hotel that wants us. That's a thing of the past," Cook recounted. Taliaferro said that he and his Indiana teammates, unlike most teams, were never split into different hotels on road trips. This would not be the case, however, when he played for the army and even later in professional football.

Despite McMillin's unfailing support of his black players, Taliaferro still had to face the color barriers that were drawn across Bloomington, Indiana, in the 1940s. After living in Gary, this was quite a culture shock. Racial tension was prevalent, even on his own football team. Taliaferro remembered a conversation he had with one teammate, an All-State football player out of Muncie, who had asked him if he was All-State as well. When Taliaferro told him he wasn't, the player wanted to know how he managed to get a scholarship without that honor. During the conversation the teammate had also made it clear that he wasn't accustomed to playing with black players. Taliaferro decided not to argue, but rather to let him see for himself why Taliaferro made the roster. He just told him, "I'll see you on the field." While no one called Taliaferro "nigger," and there were no fistfights, there were some players who Taliaferro said, "just didn't want to be bothered with me. They treated me like I was nobody, nobody." There was one player who was more vocal than others about his attitude toward the black players, Taliaferro said, but for the most part, the racism involved pretending as if the black players simply did not exist.

A racial etiquette that reinforced the idea that African Americans were second-class citizens continued to exist into the 1940s. This informal set of rules included things like refusing to shake hands, a symbol of equality, with a black person. Although it was different than the legal discrimination that existed with segregation, it could be just as devastating if not more so. It was this code of behavior that affected Taliaferro the most. The idea of being treated as if he didn't exist at all was worse to him than the more deliberate racism that included racial slurs and "separate but equal" facilities, because with those, at least he existed.

Still, the blatant forms of racism were hard on Taliaferro and his teammates. The black players on the team knew one assistant coach as the coach who would not recommend them for positions on the team. They understood that no matter how talented they were and how hard they worked, they would never do well enough to please him. His apparent prejudice was evident when classes started at Indiana University in August of 1945, just a couple of weeks after the United States dropped atomic bombs on the Japanese cities of Hiroshima and Nagasaki. The first day Taliaferro had to juggle his class schedule with football practice, he was twenty minutes late to the football field. A required class was only available at a time that conflicted with football. It ended at 3:00, the same time practice started. Although Taliaferro had tried to get into a different section, they were all closed. He had no choice but to be late to practice, as his education was his main priority. When Taliaferro showed up for practice at 3:20, he was reprimanded by this particular assistant coach. Taliaferro tried to explain why he was late, but the coach would not listen. "He just kept yelling," Taliaferro said.

Hearing about the dispute, McMillin came over to see what was going on. Unlike the assistant coach, McMillin listened to Taliaferro. "I explained the situation," Taliaferro said, "and McMillin looked at the assistant coach and told him to get me registered in a different section of the class and to get on with practice." Taliaferro was transferred into a different class section that had previously been closed. With the incident behind him Taliaferro moved on. There were other times the assistant coach said or did things purposely to get to Taliaferro and his black teammates, but Taliaferro just ignored these. He was determined not to let the assistant coach bother him. "I learned [football] from the guy and that was, after all, why I was there," Taliaferro said.

Incidents like that became motivation for Taliaferro. Every time something like that happened, it made him more determined to be successful.

He wanted to be the best athlete he could be. As an athlete, he had the opportunity to do what he couldn't do anywhere else. It was his chance "to go against the white guy," he said. It was the only way he could physically demonstrate his anger against discrimination without getting into trouble. Taliaferro fought racism the only way he could, with his performance on the athletic field.

He experienced both forms of racism at Indiana University, the form that existed in the unwritten etiquette that prevailed in race relations, and in the system of segregation that existed in Bloomington, Indiana, at the time. The optimistic outlook with which he approached life was evident in his reaction to racism in whatever form. "This was a problem they had, not a problem I had. . . . We have more things in common than we do not," Taliaferro said about race relations. "Fingers, toes, we wear clothes," he said to demonstrate his beliefs that when it comes down to it, we're all part of the same human race.

While there were people like his assistant coach who made life more difficult, there were also people who made coming to Indiana University worthwhile for Taliaferro. One such person, of course, was Coach McMillin. "Bo McMillin's interest in my welfare motivated me to stay despite all the crap," Taliaferro said. Taliaferro's support system went beyond Bo McMillin, however. There were a number of people who impacted him and motivated him to stay at Indiana University despite the racism. Another member of this support system was one of his assistant coaches, John Kovatch. Kovatch, a former Northwestern football player, was aware of the difficulty Taliaferro was experiencing adjusting to life at IU and was a constant source of support for him. Despite having a positive attitude most of the time, there were days that racism would get to Taliaferro, who wondered if he would ever be free of its limitations. In those moments Kovatch would remind Taliaferro that he was there because he was capable of contributing to the team and that he should make the best of his opportunity at Indiana University. Teammate Howard Brown was also there for him when he was at his lowest. Brown helped keep Taliaferro's attitude positive. On days he noticed Taliaferro getting down, his simple reassurances that "everything's going to be all right" kept Taliaferro going.

There was also a support system made up of the African American students on campus. Whether undergraduate or graduate students, they stuck together. Lehman Adams, a graduate student and Taliaferro's friend, explained how these relationships formed, "How do you become friends when you're a few black students among thousands? . . . You become friends—

The coaching staff of the 1945 Hoosiers from left to right: Charles McDaniel, John Kovatch, Alvin "Bo" McMillin, Paul "Pooch" Harrell, and Gordon Fisher. Harrell was the head baseball coach at Indiana University from 1939 through 1947. *Photo courtesy IU Archives.*

you're forced to!" Being a member of Kappa Alpha Psi fraternity also provided support for Taliaferro during these times. Founded in 1911 at Indiana University, the purpose of the fraternity was to help the few black students who were not only rejected by the white majority on campus and in town but who were also dissuaded from remaining there. Kappa Alpha Psi's mission was to provide the support needed for black male students on campus to remain there and become successful despite the many obstacles put in their

Indiana University assistant football coach John Kovatch, a former Northwestern gridder, in 1945. Kovatch helped Taliaferro adjust to life in segregated Bloomington, Indiana, in the 1940s. *Photo courtesy IU Archives.*

way. More than three decades after its founding, this mission continued to help black students on campus, students like George Taliaferro, who, like their predecessors, continued to face racism and segregation.

The Kappa Alpha Psi fraternity house was nothing more than a kitchen and dining area, but fraternity brothers who lived in the house actually lived in its rooms because everyone ate at the home of John and Ruth Mays, the unofficial union building for black students. While Taliaferro never resided in the fraternity house, he was an active member of the organization. He needed reassurance and he needed friends, not just because of what he was going through with teammates, but also because of what he was experiencing living in a segregated Bloomington. The east side of town, the "gown" side, was the university half of the town. The "town" side was just that, the town side. The line drawn between the two also marked the color line in Bloomington, with African Americans limited to the "town" side. There was a covenant in Bloomington at the time, Taliaferro said, that black people could not live on the east side of town.

The black football players, including Taliaferro, lived at 418 East 8th Street, the home of John and Ruth Mays. Taliaferro was sitting on the steps of this home on August 15, the day Japan surrendered to the Allies, marking the end of World War II. The Mays' home, just off campus, was considered to be on the "gown" side of town. Because black students were not housed on campus, homes off campus, like the Mays' home, and the Lincoln House, where black female students lived, were authorized by IU president Wells as university facilities. They had the same rules as the dorms on campus and black students on scholarship, like Taliaferro, were given a monthly stipend to pay for their room and board since they weren't permitted to live in the official dorms. The room and board of the white students on scholarship went through the bursar's office like the rest of the money for tuition and books. Taliaferro's stipend for room and board was $52 a month. He paid around $40 a month to Mr. and Mrs. Mays. This left him plenty of money, he said, for his other living expenses.

A family home that had been converted, the Mays' was home to single, black male students. The diminutive house held anywhere from 12 to 16 people, three or four people in each small room, rooms that could only comfortably fit two people. It was also rumored that there were a couple of ghosts living in the basement, although Taliaferro never made the trip down the dank basement steps to verify their existence. Also, because black students were not welcome at restaurants on campus, the Mays' home had become the unofficial hangout and cafeteria, meaning even more people were often crowded into what was already a very small space.

Making the living situation more interesting was Mr. Mays. He was always angry and, Taliaferro said, "He drank anything he could get his hands on, and he was always going to put somebody out. He'd say 'I'll put you out of here!'" Mrs. Mays, the reverse of her husband, "was an angel," Taliaferro said. She would just shake her head when her husband started yelling. Taliaferro and the other football players quickly learned to pay Mr. Mays little attention. "He was so much smaller than most of us anyway," he explained. The threats never amounted to any more than just that, Taliaferro continued. Despite the cramped quarters and drama, Taliaferro considered himself lucky for having a room at the Mays' home. Black men who did not get a spot there had to live on the west side of Bloomington, the "town" side, farther from campus.

Lehman Adams was one of the unlucky ones who did not get a spot at the Mays' home. He arrived on campus before classes started so he could find a place to live. Although he tried everywhere, he could not find an available room anywhere in the segregated town. Desperate and having already registered for classes, he went to an adviser to ask for help. That got him nowhere. The adviser explained that there simply were no other options because he wasn't permitted to live on campus. If there were no places on the town side for Adams to rent, he was told, he might just have to go back home. The adviser, who didn't seem to be too concerned with Adams's problem, said there was nothing he could do. Although angry, disappointed, and frustrated, Adams was not deterred. He was determined to attend IU and get an education, so he spent the night at a different friend's house each night until he finally found a room to rent in the private home of an African American couple. While he was happy to have found living arrangements, living on the west side was difficult for students like Adams. He had to walk about four miles from the 900 block on the west side of town, to the 800 block on the east side of town every day, rain or snow, to get to his classes.

Equally difficult for black students at Indiana University was finding a place to eat. It was especially difficult for those who did not live in the Lincoln House or the Mays' home. For meals, they either had to leave campus and go back to the west side of town or eat at the Mays' home. There was no restaurant on the east side of town, the "gown" side, which welcomed black customers. The Mays' home was closer than going to the west side of town, but was still a couple of miles from campus. Every meal was a hassle for Indiana University's black students. Taliaferro understood that his was a more fortunate situation than most. Still, it bothered him that he had been actively recruited by a university where he was not permitted to live in the university dorms and where he had a hard time getting his meals. It just wasn't right. He knew it, and it gnawed at him every time he ate a meal in Bloomington.

Every day at lunch, for example, Taliaferro would have to walk from his class at University School, across the extensive campus, to the Mays' home, where he would have to scarf down his food. He didn't even have time to talk. He barely had time to sit down. Although he shoved the food in his mouth as quickly as he could, he still had to sprint the two miles back to campus to make it to his next class on time. Getting a haircut was no easier. The barbershop was located next to the segregated Princess Theater. Despite being owned by a black man, Mr. Shawntee, and being just a few blocks from the Mays' home, Taliaferro was not permitted inside. Because it was located on the "gown" side of Bloomington, Taliaferro had to make an appointment instead to go to Mr. Shawntee's home. Because his home was located on the west side, getting a haircut meant a three-mile walk instead of the three-block walk it should have been.

"That was my world. Small world. Very small," Taliaferro said. But to him, those were the inconveniences he had to put up with in order to get an education. In order to deal with his frustration so that it didn't consume him, he had to find something positive in the experience. Dealing with the racism and segregation that existed in Bloomington may have actually kept the black students from flunking out of the university, he decided. "We didn't have any place to go or anything to do, and, therefore we studied." The black students would get together, sometimes having dances and parties at one of the private homes they lived in, but they were so confined by space and location that they simply could not do too much socializing, something that had been detrimental to some of the white students. "I cannot remember a black student failing at Indiana University when I was at school. Being discriminated in Bloomington, Indiana, was a small price for me to pay to get a quality education. It has prepared me for the world," Taliaferro explained. In an article by Bob Hammel, Taliaferro says, "There were things I couldn't do and places I couldn't go. But I didn't let anything stand between me and playing football. I made up my mind 'If I can't go there, I can go to class.'"

Although Bloomington was segregated and Taliaferro was not able to live in the dorm with his white teammates, in many ways Indiana University seemed to be ahead of other major Indiana schools. Neither Purdue nor Notre Dame had black players in their football programs in 1945. At Indiana University, however, there had been black football players since Preston

The studious side of George Taliaferro in December 1945. At Indiana University on a football scholarship, he said racism was "a small price to pay" for the education he received. *Photo courtesy IU Archives.*

Eagleson became the first to play both football and baseball for the Hoosiers in 1890. Eagleson started what Herman B Wells, George Taliaferro, and Bo McMillin would continue. On a trip to another Indiana college, Eagleson was denied accommodations in a hotel because of his race. He filed suit against the hotel and received damages, setting a precedent in Indiana. He set another precedent by becoming the first black man to receive a graduate degree from Indiana University when he received a Master of Arts degree in philosophy. Like Taliaferro, Eagleson understood that education was the means to his self-determination.

The Eagleson family continued to fight social injustice, according to a book by Frances V. Halsell Gilliam, when Eagleson's younger brother attended IU in 1921. Halston Eagleson, Jr., didn't play football, but played in the band instead. Probably to prevent him from earning his letter sweater, he was kidnapped on his way to Lafayette, Indiana, for the 1922 football game at Purdue. He was taken to Spencer, Indiana, and jailed. The kidnapping managed to keep Eagleson from getting to Lafayette for the game, and thus from earning his letter sweater, an honor the kidnappers apparently did not want bestowed on a black man. It wasn't until 1982 that a retired Halston Eagleson was finally awarded his sweater.

Aside from Preston Eagleson, there were other early black football players for IU. Jesse Babb, a halfback and Fitzhugh Lyons, an end, both played for the Crimson from 1931 to 1933. This tradition continued at IU, and in 1945, under Coach McMillin, George Taliaferro and Mel Groomes were starting for the Hoosiers, and other black players were on the roster—including Bill Buckner, whose son Quinn was to be a Hall of Fame basketball player and a two-year football starter at IU.

Indiana University Football

1945 was a volatile time for college football. College teams everywhere lost players to the wartime draft. Many, however, also had World War II veterans playing on their teams. Similar problems plagued the National Football League. Attendance at NFL games dropped during the war, and there was a shortage of players. According to Robert W. Peterson's *Pigskin: The Early Years of Pro Football,* 638 active NFL players had gone into the armed forces by the war's end. Of these player/soldiers, 355 were officers, 66 were decorated, and 21 were killed, according to the NFL encyclopedia. Because of the loss of players and coaches (even George Halas was called up for Navy duty in the middle of the 1942 season), the team limit was cut from 33 to 25, and an unlimited substitutions rule was implemented. Even with these regulations in place, however, some teams still did not have enough players to field a team. In 1943, for example, the Cleveland Rams suspended operations for the season because of the shortage. Some teams avoided shutting down by merging with another team in order to have enough players. The Philadelphia Eagles and the Pittsburgh Steelers, for example, merged for one season under the name Phil-Pitt Steagles. Two years later, the Brooklyn Tigers and Boston Yanks merged for the 1945 season. Nothing, it seems, was certain for football, and college football in 1945 was no exception.

Even with the changes, it is fair to say that many people were not expecting a season like the one Indiana University ended up having. The night before their first game of the season, Coach McMillin held a team dinner. Not everyone was there. Pete Pihos, the fullback who would go on to Professional Football Hall of Fame status, wouldn't return from military service until late September. Howard Brown and Charlie Armstrong were also still in the service. Among those present, however, were Ben Raimondi, the quarterback, and Mel Groomes, a halfback. The ends were Bob Ravensberg and Ted Kluszewski. McMillin's "po' li'l boys" were actually a very talented group of individuals.

According to Hammel and Klingelhoffer in *Glory of Old IU,* Ravensberg was the only consensus All-American selection on the team. Quarterback Ben Raimondi, however, was a strong quarterback. Years later when he was rated using the NCAA grading system, his pass rating was high: 145.1. Ted Kluszewski's skills weren't limited to football. Kluszewski, who also played baseball for the Hurryin' Hoosiers, was noticed by the Cincinnati Reds when the two baseball teams shared practice facilities. Wartime restrictions had forced the Reds to do their spring training in Bloomington from 1943 through 1945. Kluszewski's batting average at IU, despite having only played sandlot ball until that point, was .443. Taliaferro said, "And he didn't just hit the ball—he crushed it!" The Reds, Taliaferro said, witnessed one of Kluszewski's power hits—the ball was hit onto the HPER building, quite a distance from where he was batting, for an easy homerun. "They signed him the next day," Taliaferro said. Kluszewski, the "quiet man" as his teammates referred to him, stood 6'3" and weighed about 235 pounds. Taliaferro said, "His biceps were the size of most people's thighs, and he could just as successfully have played professional football as pro baseball." If that is the case, he would have been an impressive tight end in the NFL, because his statistics with the Reds are impressive. He played for 15 seasons, three times hitting at least 40 home runs and three times hitting more home runs than he had strikeouts. He was so successful that in 1998 the Cincinnati Reds retired his jersey, #18, and when they built a new stadium, a statue of "Big Klu" went up outside. Although he would eventually be one of Cincinnati's most popular baseball players, he still had one Indiana football season to play.

Linemen John Goldsberry and Russ Deal, Bob Meyer, center, and tackle Joe Sowinski were also at the team dinner that night and part of the talent pool McMillin had collected. The team had been preparing for the game all week, so the dinner was more of a bonding experience than game preparation. McMillin used the opportunity to discuss an idea with Taliaferro.

"Are you a superstitious person?" McMillin asked him in his Texan drawl.

"Not really," Taliaferro replied. McMillin was, however, and he told Taliaferro that he wanted to change his jersey number from 43 to 44.

Billy Hillenbrand and Vern Huffman previously had worn the #44 jersey, McMillin explained. Huffman was the 1936 Big Ten MVP. He was also the only IU athlete to win All-American honors in two sports, football and basketball. Billy Hillenbrand was IU's all-time punt return leader and he was also an All-American. Taliaferro figured McMillin wanted him to wear the same number because he saw something special in Taliaferro as well; maybe he thought Taliaferro was also destined to be an All-American.

'That's fine with me," Taliaferro said. In fact, he would consider it an honor. After his initial doubts about becoming a part of the team, to be asked to wear the number of two of Indiana's All-Americans was a compliment Taliaferro didn't take lightly.

The next day, September 22, 1945, Taliaferro was ready to wear his new number in his first college football game. The first challenge of the game had been in getting there. Having no bus, the team had to borrow gas-rationing stamps and travel the day before the game in about 30 cars to Ann Arbor, Michigan. In the visitors' locker room the next day, Taliaferro geared up for the game. He put on his #44 jersey and listened to McMillin's locker-room talk. McMillin, known for his fiery inspirational speeches, had managed to bring his players to tears on more than one occasion. Nobody cried after his Michigan locker-room talk, but the Cream and Crimson were fired up and ready to play. When it was finally game time, Taliaferro ran onto the field and looked up at the tallest, widest stadium he had ever seen. Of course, it was packed full of loud Michigan Wolverine fans. An eighteen-year-old freshman who was playing with and against returning war veterans in their twenties, he couldn't help but be intimidated. To add to the pressure, he was one of the starting 11. He was a freshman starting as a tailback and halfback, something that wouldn't happen again at IU for 49 years. He was worried that he would let the team down.

Being young and inexperienced wasn't a factor once Taliaferro received his first hit, his initiation to college football. "Once you get hit, you forget about everything else," he said. After that, his desire to play was all that mattered. "Nobody ever enjoyed playing football any more than I did. I lived to play football. It was that much fun," he said. Still, this was the first game of the season, and it would prove to be a challenge for the young Hoosiers. Michigan Stadium was a place where "historically visiting teams' hopes of unbeaten seasons have died," Hammel and Klingelhoffer wrote. To make matters worse, they added, the Indiana University Hoosiers had actually defeated Michigan at Michigan Stadium the previous year, 20 to 0, so Michigan was sure to be out for blood. It wasn't the Oaken Bucket, but it was a serious rivalry nevertheless, and not a game to be taken lightly.

In the first quarter Taliaferro ran for 14 yards to put Indiana on Michigan's 39-yard line. He then passed 14 yards to end Ted Kluszewski to put Indiana on the Michigan 25. On the next play, he ran through Michigan's line for a 13-yard gain and then managed to make it into the end zone "shaking off tacklers," according to Jack Overmyer, the Hoosiers' press director. This first touchdown, wrote Hammel in a Bloomington *Herald-Times* article, came on a 56-yard drive in the first quarter that "introduced the Wolverines to Talia-ferro." As spectacular as it was, a holding penalty cost the Indiana Hoosiers the touchdown and put them back on the 15. This didn't stop Taliaferro, who threw a screen pass to Dick Deranek on the next play. Then quarterback Ben Raimondi threw a pass to Kluszewski, who took it into the end zone. The second Hoosier touchdown came on an 81-yard drive by Nick Sebek, Mel Groomes, and Ben Raimondi, giving the Hoosiers a 13 to 0 lead.

Despite a valiant effort by the Wolverines, their only score came on an Indiana blunder. In the third quarter, Michigan capitalized on a short punt by Taliaferro to the Hoosiers' own 49, making the score 13 to 7. Indiana managed to hold onto its lead until there were only two minutes to go. The Bomen, as Bo McMillin's team was sometimes called, were still leading 13 to 7, but Michigan had the ball on the Hoosier 8-yard line, along with the op-portunity to take the lead and the game from the visitors. Hammel described what happened next. He wrote: "Two running plays advanced the ball to the four. A third try didn't advance it. . . . On fourth down, the Wolverines took too much time getting a play set and backed up to the nine. There, with fifty-five seconds left, they lined up in field-goal formation. It was a fake. Indiana played for it and stuffed the play, killing the threat and clinching victory." When the game was over, Indiana had won 13 to 7 and had set in motion an astonishing season.

For his debut and despite his initial qualms, Taliaferro did not disappoint McMillin, who had entrusted him with a starting position and lucky jer-sey. Of Taliaferro's introductory performance Hammel wrote: "Taliaferro didn't score but did everything else in as spectacular and crucial a debut as an eighteen-year-old ever had." It was after this Michigan game that Talia-ferro began to realize he was establishing himself as a starter. "When I played football against the University of Michigan and won, I said, 'This is different. In the history of Indiana University, this is different,'" he said. Perhaps that was because Taliaferro ran for 95 yards in 20 carries and completed three of three passes for 23 yards. He would have debuted with a 100-yard game if he hadn't taken a loss to run out the clock on the last play of the game. Taliaferro's impressive initiation into college football was not perfect, however. Hammel noted that he had botched a couple of punts and that when McMillin asked what happened, Taliaferro had replied, "I was too scared to know."

The Northwestern game came next, on September 29. Pete Pihos and Howard Brown, who had been in the service for two years, were back from the war and back to Indiana football. According to Hammel and Klingelhoffer, the two were back on a 60-day leave having come back from impressive stints in the military. "Pihos won a battlefield promotion to Lieutenant with General George Patton's 35th Infantry Division in bloody fighting in Europe during World War II. Brown won three purple hearts in the same war theater," they wrote. Pihos and Brown only had a couple of practices with their teammates before the game, but whether their football skills were rusty or not, they were going to be needed. Despite a strong season opener against Michigan without two of their key players, Indiana was going to struggle against Northwestern. Also, the Hoosier center, Bob Meyer, had broken his leg during the Michigan game. John Cannady, who had hopes of being a linebacker, was to step in at center. According to Hammel and Klingelhoffer, Cannady said: "It rained. I had never snapped the ball in the rain. The morning of the game at our hotel, Bo took me upstairs with the backs. He put six footballs in the bathtub. A coach would hand one to me, I'd snap it to the quarterback, and they ran plays right there in the room." Taliaferro said Cannady was a natural at the position and continued at center for the Hoosiers; on defense, he remained at linebacker.

Taliaferro's performance wasn't quite what it was in the Michigan game. Northwestern outplayed the Hoosiers for the first three quarters and had the only touchdown, which came from a blocked Taliaferro punt. And although Taliaferro had carried 19 times for 77 yards, he had also lost 21 yards for a net of only 56. Still, the Hoosiers managed to score one in the fourth. Passes to Groomes and Ravensberg advanced the Bomen to the Northwestern 15-yard line. McMillin put in Pihos and Brown. On the next play, Raimondi passed to Pihos who caught the ball at the five and powered through three Northwestern defenders, who he dragged with him into the end zone for the score. Charlie Armstrong's place kick would be the tie. Armstrong had also just come back from the war. A bomber pilot who, according to Hammel and Klingelhoffer, was decorated with the Distinguished Flying Cross, he had been intent on quitting football and getting a commercial pilot's license. Luckily for the Hoosiers, he changed his mind and decided to play another season of football. His kick, right on target, saved the Cream and Crimson from near defeat, ending the game in a frustrating tie, which McMillin lik-

The 1945 Hoosier starting backs. In the front row is Ben Raimondi. Back row from left is Mel Groomes, Pete Pihos, and George Taliaferro. Pihos and Taliaferro would eventually be inducted into the College Football Hall of Fame. *Photo courtesy IU Archives.*

ened to "getting a kiss from your sister." It wasn't a win, but it wasn't a loss, something that would be more important as the season wore on. Taliaferro said it was an important game because of the addition of Pihos and Brown. Although they had beat Michigan without them, Taliaferro knew that having them on the team made it that much stronger.

The Hoosiers fared better in the October 6 game against Illinois. The first score for the Cream and Crimson came in the fourth quarter, despite two completions into the end zone during the second quarter. For the first, Raimondi had thrown to Kluszewski in the end zone, but the play was called back when the Illini band's mascot, a dog, trotted onto the field. The same play a second time yielded the same results when the officials ruled that Kluszewski had stepped out of bounds. Taliaferro was held in check until the fourth quarter, which the Hoosiers started by taking the ball on a penalty at the Illinois 42. A couple of Taliaferro running plays and some complete passes put the Hoosiers on the 10. This time, the Raimondi pass to Kluszewski in the end zone wasn't called back, and the Hoosiers had the winning touchdown.

Twenty-two thousand people showed up at Indiana's Memorial Stadium for the October 13 homecoming game against Nebraska, and they did not leave disappointed. The Bomen donned their red home jerseys with white numbers for this game. Although the colors are cream and crimson, they wore black pants with a white stripe down the side and black helmets. The helmets were made of padded leather, and there were no face masks. It was Taliaferro's first game at Indiana's horseshoe-shaped 10th Street Stadium. Once considered one of the premier college playing fields, the stadium was the setting of many memorable Indiana University football games. The Nebraska game was no exception. By halftime, Taliaferro had helped his team to a 27 to 0 lead. Hoosier halfback Bob Miller ran a 95-yard kickoff return to start the second half with another touchdown. Reserves finished the game; everyone got to play, and the Cream and Crimson managed a 54 to 14 victory. The Nebraska Cornhuskers, on the other hand, had only managed to cross the 50-yard line twice during the entire second half of the game.

The Hoosiers racked up more points against Iowa the following week. Taliaferro, the "Gary flash," contributed with some big touchdown runs, one for 63 yards and again later down the sideline for 74 yards. By the third quarter, the substitutes were in, but the Hoosiers still managed to score a whopping 52 points and their third Big Ten victory of the season. The Hawkeyes had managed to score 20 points, but it wasn't enough to overcome the offensive might of the Hurryin' Hoosiers.

Despite his two amazing runs against Iowa, the Tulsa game was even more memorable for Taliaferro. Before the game, Indiana had two consecutive 50-point wins. But Tulsa, also undefeated, was not going to go down quite so easily. It was a contest of two of the best college football teams of 1945 playing head-to-head. The game, Taliaferro said, was "what college football is about: blocking, tackling, defense, and teamwork." After several punts, the first score of the game came in the second quarter. It started with

George Taliaferro, #44, carries the ball during the Indiana/Tulsa game on October 27, 1945. Both teams were undefeated going into the game, but Indiana came out with a 7 to 2 win. During this game some of Tulsa's players made it clear that they didn't appreciate playing against black players. They lost their captain early in the game for roughing up Taliaferro. *Photo courtesy IU Archives.*

a Mel Groomes pass to Taliaferro for a considerable gain. On the next play, Indiana's end, Bob Ravensberg, on a pass from fullback Pete Pihos, got into the end zone. Tulsa managed to score only 2 points when they scored a safety by tackling Taliaferro in his own end zone. Strong defense from both teams left the remaining action scoreless, though not without nail biting, and the game ended with a hard-fought Indiana win, 7 to 2.

"That was one of my best games," Taliaferro said, notwithstanding the safety. The Tulsa game, however, was memorable for another reason as well. In *Hoosier Autumn,* a book about the 1945 Hoosier football team, Robert

D. Arnold wrote, "After a few plays, it was obvious that the Tulsa players didn't appreciate playing against blacks." Tulsa, Arnold wrote, actually lost their captain, C. B. Stanley, early in the game for roughing up Taliaferro. Mel Groomes, another black player, was also targeted, but Taliaferro seemed to be the receiver of the bulk of Tulsa's antics.

With much less drama, the Hoosiers beat Cornell on November 3 at Memorial Stadium 46 to 6. The fact that Coach Bo McMillin was absent in order to scout the Minnesota Golden Gophers and that the starters rested much of the game to avoid injury in order to be strong for the Minnesota game mattered little. Although he didn't play as much as he usually did, Taliaferro still managed to contribute a touchdown to the win.

As the season progressed, Taliaferro played an increasingly larger role in his team's wins. His triple-threat skills, which would, in time, propel him into professional football, were a key contribution to the team's success. Taliaferro, who played tailback for the Hoosiers and had secured his star position on the team when he ran two consecutive 80-yard touchdown runs in practice, was not a disappointment to McMillin, and his skills were noticed on campus as well. His popularity on campus increased with every game. Even at a time of prevalent racism, he was often approached for his autograph while walking along campus between classes. His good nature and charm made him accessible, and he would happily oblige the autograph seekers. McMillin had not been overstating Taliaferro's position on the team when he reassured him that first day.

McMillin was actually one of his biggest fans, as Sam Banks, a writer for *Our Sports* magazine, illustrated in an article about Taliaferro. Apparently Coach McMillin was having his usual coffee break one morning when Taliaferro and a couple of other players stopped by to see him. It wasn't out of the ordinary for them to stop in. They respected McMillin, whose conduct as both a coach and person had encouraged and inspired them, and they considered him not only a coach, but also a friend and mentor. During the visit, however, the football players started to mess with each other. "As kids will do, they were wrestling on the stairs and George slipped and fell flat on his back," Banks wrote. McMillin rolled his eyes up as if in prayer and then ran to Taliaferro's side. As soon as he got to him, Taliaferro rolled over laughing and jumped up to his feet. McMillin didn't seem to think it was too funny. "Boy, don't you ever do that to me again. Why, you're my bread and butter," he told Taliaferro.

Although McMillin seemed to be joking, there was some truth to his statement. At the season's end, Taliaferro would make All Big Ten as a fresh-

Bo McMillin, who saw talent, not color, rests his hand on George Taliaferro's knee. McMillin, who recruited, played, and started black players, refused to stay in hotels that did not welcome his black players. From left: Pete Pihos, Coach Alvin "Bo" McMillin, George Taliaferro, Bob Harbison. *Photo courtesy George Taliaferro.*

man at Indiana and he would lead the Hoosiers in rushing with 719 yards (he averaged 4.5 yards a carry and had six touchdowns). He would also lead the Hoosiers in punting with 1,315 yards, averaging almost 33 yards a punt. He was the only Big Ten back to average more than 100 yards a game running and passing. While statistics may give some indication as to ability, however, to see him in action was more thrilling, and there were plenty of people on hand for the memorable game against Minnesota to witness his football aptitude.

On the way to the game, Coach McMillin noticed a white horse in a field. Ever superstitious, he immediately licked his finger and stamped it in his other hand for good luck. They were going to need it. Indiana had only won two of its last 50 games against Minnesota, and the low temperature was going to make for a game the Hoosiers wouldn't forget. At home, the Minnesota Golden Gophers could usually count on the weather to play a factor in the game's outcome. Other teams simply were not used to playing in the extreme weather found in Minnesota during football season, an obvious advantage for the Gophers. Stan Sutton wrote that the Minnesota weather "would keep a postman from finishing his route," and that "Minneapolis winters were cold enough to make penguins shiver."

While back in Indiana the temperature on this November day hovered around 60 degrees, Minnesota was a different story, according to Taliaferro. A snowstorm and freezing temperatures met the Hoosiers, whose uniforms and coats provided little relief from the cold. It was exactly the kind of weather that put Minnesota at a serious advantage, earning it the title of "twelfth man." Before the game had even started, Taliaferro was jumping around, trying to keep his muscles warm. It wasn't working, though, and he could feel his muscles tightening as he stood and looked at the field. It was going to be a very long game, he thought. It may have surprised the Gophers to hear that Taliaferro was having a problem coping with the weather, since he started the game with a 97-yard kickoff return to the Minnesota three. In the Sutton article, Taliaferro said, "I was absolutely running in place. When I got to the 3 one of the biggest players on the Minnesota team caught me and knocked me down." His fumble on the next play, recovered by Minnesota, may have been more along the lines of what the Gophers were expecting, or at least hoping for. The play was supposed to be a snap to Taliaferro, but it went too far left and Taliaferro lost it. The opposition didn't see many of those kinds of mistakes from the Hoosiers, though, as Taliaferro and company continued to astonish the Gopher defense despite the sub-zero-degree weather.

The bone-chilling temperatures didn't keep Taliaferro from scoring three touchdowns and making a 90-yard interception return. McMillin took him out, to Taliaferro's delight, to give him a break after the third touchdown. By the time the game had ended, the Hoosiers hadn't just beaten the Golden Gophers, they had handed Minnesota, a team that had won five national championships between 1934 and 1941, a 49 to 0 thumping, in their home stadium in weather conditions only they could truly appreciate. The Gophers had contributed to the Hoosier win by throwing six interceptions, but the Hoosiers were well-prepared for the match.

The combination of coaching and playing talent earned the Hoosiers an astonishing season. The Bomen continued their season with another shutout against Pittsburgh on November 17, 19 to 0. The Hoosiers were on their way to an undefeated season with only the Purdue game to be played. The

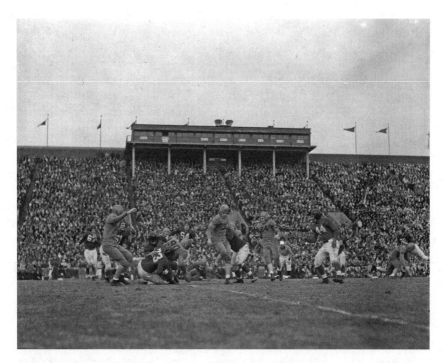

During the November 10, 1945, game in Minnesota, Taliaferro and the Hoosiers managed to overcome Minnesota's twelfth man, the bitter cold, to continue their winning streak. During the game Taliaferro scored three touchdowns and made a 90-yard interception return. The Hoosiers won the game 49 to 0. *Photo courtesy IU Archives.*

Cream and Crimson topped off the season on November 24, 1945, at the 48th Old Oaken Bucket game against their archrival, the Purdue Boilermakers. On hand to watch the historic match were 26,000 zealous fans. Unlike other Oaken Bucket games, however, this one was missing one key element, The Battle of the Bands. This traditional halftime feature, a battle between the rival marching bands, had to be cancelled because Indiana's nationally acclaimed band "The Marching Hundred" was missing too many members due to the war. The Hoosiers had been fortunate to keep their band together as long as they had. Other universities had been faced with the same problem, and some had been forced to give up their bands altogether.

Despite the lack of halftime entertainment, at least the game would be played. There were some serious attempts to score from both sides, but the

An aerial view of 10th Street Stadium on November 24, 1945, during the last game of the season against Purdue. Approximately 27,000 fans watched the Hoosiers beat Purdue and earn the coveted Old Oaken Bucket Trophy, an undefeated season, and the first undisputed Big Ten championship in the school's history. *Photo courtesy IU Archives.*

first half ended with both teams still at zero. The Boilermakers had fought to keep up with the Hoosiers, but they had nothing left to give after that. By the time the second half got under way, the Black and Gold was out of steam and no match for the Hoosier might. Taliaferro, Pihos, and Groomes helped get the ball to the Purdue 31. Then Raimondi passed to Taliaferro who made it to the 1 yard line. Pihos made it into the end zone on his second attempt for the first IU touchdown. A Kluszewski interception led to another Pihos score before the third quarter ended. Two more Raimondi touchdown passes, to Kluszewski and Louis Mihajlovich, added another 13 points in the fourth. The Hoosiers, as had so often been the case during that '45 season, dominated the game. The victory over Purdue meant the Hoosiers had managed not just a win, but an undisputed Big Ten championship, an undefeated season, and an Old Oaken Bucket trophy. The tie against Northwestern, 7 to 7, was the only glitch in an otherwise perfect season.

An *Indianapolis Star* program honoring the unbeaten team described the end of the game: "As the final shot ended the game, hundreds of fans rushed onto the field, caught Bo in the avalanche and hurried him off to the Hoosiers' quarters." It went on to describe the scene in the locker room: "And the dressing room which was busier than a well-stocked cigarette counter during the war shortage, all was confusion, but everyone knew that Indi-

John Goldsberry, Russell Deal, Bob Ravensberg, and George Taliaferro read "Hail the Champs" on January 10, 1946. The *Indianapolis Star* sponsored the brochure which celebrated Indiana University's conference championship and undefeated season. An emotionally over-whelmed Bo McMillin appears on the cover. On the back is a list of Indiana Hoosier football players and former players who served in World War II. *Photo courtesy IU Archives.*

ana beat Purdue." Many fans remained in the locker room, still cheering their Cream and Crimson heroes. Among those, the program indicated, was McMillin's own mentor from his grammar school days in Texas, Robert Myers, McMillin's first football coach. Myers asked McMillin which underdog win had been more thrilling for him, when he led Centre to beat Harvard, or Indiana's defeat of Purdue that day. McMillin replied without hesitation that the Indiana game had been the more thrilling. To sweeten the victory,

President Herman Wells, also in the locker room, cancelled classes the following Monday and decided to have a convocation later in the week for the student body to celebrate.

In a ceremony after the game, another "I" was added to the Oaken Bucket to celebrate Indiana's 26 to 0 shutout victory over Purdue. A poem written by Carl Lewis explains the bucket's glory: "I'm called the 'old' oaken bucket, but I can never be old. I live with youth and will as long as there are young men to vie for my favor one November day of each year." The Hoosiers could not have scripted a better ending to their perfect season than earning the coveted trophy. After the game, Russell "Mutt" Deal's Indiana teammates voted the decorated World War II veteran the permanent captain of the team. It was Deal's fourth game against Purdue and fourth victory over this rival.

So, under the leadership of Coach McMillin and Russell Deal, in 1945, Indiana University, with a record of 9-0-1, had an undefeated football season for the first and only time in the school's history. The football team also won an undisputed Big Ten championship for the first time, though this powerful conference was actually called the Western Conference or "Big Nine" at the time. The University of Chicago had been part of the conference, but had dropped out, thus earning the new nickname. Although it remained the Big Nine the entire time Taliaferro played for Indiana, many people still referred to the conference as the Big Ten. Later, when Michigan State joined the conference, it became the Big Ten again. Regardless, Indiana had won an undisputed Big Ten championship.

"It can happen. A football team wallowing in the muck of mediocrity suddenly takes off and soars, higher than it has ever flown before. And then almost as abruptly it descends, never to repeat its journey," Mark Montieth wrote in a 1995 *Indianapolis Star* article about that 1945 football season. "Call it kismet, karma, destiny, or anything you like. It's what happens when talent, effort and good fortune merge for one brief shining moment to produce something that borders on perfection," he continued.

Yet some critics, who apparently did not believe in kismet, karma, or destiny, credited World War II with Indiana's perfect season. Coach McMillin did not take kindly to such suggestions. He was rather insulted at the idea. He believed his "po' l'il boys" simply had the determination and talent to make it happen. Apparently he was not the only one to think so. Five of his starters had earned recognition. Bob Ravensberg was named All-American first team, second team, and All-Big Ten second team. Pete Pihos was named All-American second team and All-Big Ten first team. Ted Kluszewski was named All-Big Ten first team, and John Goldsberry was named All-Big Ten second team. Freshman Taliaferro also racked up the honors. On top of this, the Indiana University football program earned, along with a conference championship, a fourth-place ranking in the Associated Press football poll. In first, second, and third place were Army, Navy, and Alabama's Crimson Tide. The Hoosiers were in good company. Adding to the accolades was Bo McMillin, who was named Coach of the Year.

McMillin would have liked IU to get a chance to play number one–ranked Army, and there actually had been talk of a post-season game between the two greats. Hammel and Klingelhoffer explained that Big Ten rules prohibited post-season play for its teams, but that there was a movement for a bowl match-up between Army and Indiana at Soldier Field for war relief. As many as 125,000 people were expected to attend what was sure to be a battle. Apparently, General Eisenhower denied permission, saying the cadets had to study for their mid-term exams. However, McMillin was confident his Hoosiers could have taken the popular Army team. According to Hammel and Klingelhoffer, McMillin said in a speech at his Coach of the Year dinner, "I haven't seen Blanchard but until I do, I'll settle for Pete Pihos any time. . . . I've heard a lot about DeWitt Coulter, Army's wonderful left tackle. I never saw Coulter play, but until I have, I'll take John Goldsberry, our 230-pound left tackle and the fastest man on our line." He continued, "Maybe you've never heard of Ted Kluszewski and Bob Ravensberg, our ends. They were the best ends Fritz Crisler of Michigan saw all season, by his own quotes. . . . Our line was probably the best in the Big Ten in 10 years, the real secret of our unbeaten season and Big Ten championship. That line allowed only one touchdown all season, and that was by Michigan in the first game, before Brown, Cannady and Pihos were in the lineup." McMillin didn't stop there. "It was a hell of a line. . . . It's too bad Army had a full schedule. We'd have loved to meet them," he drawled.

Although the two teams never got a chance to play, that didn't keep people from debating who would have won. Hammel and Klingelhoffer pointed to the Michigan games, which were the only true comparisons that could be made of the two football teams. Indiana had beaten the Wolverines 13 to 7, while Army beat the Wolverines by a slightly larger margin, 28 to 7. Still, that wasn't a true comparison, because the Indiana/Michigan game, the first game of the season, was before the return of two key Indiana players, Pete Pihos and Howard Brown. Who would have won a contest between the two teams is anybody's guess. Hoosier fans no doubt believed the Bomen could have taken a tough Army team. The only thing that wasn't up for debate was that it would have been one heck of a game.

The end of the 1945 college football season signaled a new beginning for professional football. At the same time that IU was winning the championship, the National Football League was emerging as a force in professional sports. Robert Peterson, author of *Pigskin: The Early Years of Pro Football,* wrote that by the end of the 1945 season, pro players, like their college counterparts, were starting to return to their teams after having served in World War II. NFL fans were also beginning to make a return. In 1942, attendance had dropped to about 900,000. In 1945, however, an attendance record was set with 1,918,631 fans enjoying professional football, an average of 28,636 for the season's 68 games and a big boost from 1942. Things were beginning to look up for the war-scarred league.

The league was evolving because of the war, but was bringing with it a new tradition for the same reason. A pre-game event that had started as a show of patriotism during the war became a permanent part of the NFL and athletic competition tradition. Peterson wrote: "During the war, playing the national anthem had become a ceremonial prelude to NFL games." Even though the war was over, the commissioner felt that the anthem should continue to be played before each game. Peterson quoted Commissioner Elmer Layden's announcement in his book: "It should be as much a part of every game as the kickoff. We must not drop it simply because the war is over. We should never forget what it stands for." A 1945 *Newsweek* article, Peterson wrote, also predicted positive changes for professional football. Peterson quoted *Newsweek* columnist John Lardner: "The end of the war may be the event which will build the sport into national proportions both geographically and commercially, just as the end of the last war gave pro players their original impetus and made them begin to think of organization and responsibility." The war was over, bringing changes to the world and to professional football. Lardner was right. There were big changes in store for professional football, and George Taliaferro would eventually be a significant part of them.

George Taliaferro was a letter winner his freshman year. He was a major contributor to Indiana's football glory, including being named the league's best all-around offensive player, Associated Press first team Big Ten, and second team All-American by the *Sporting News.* He was also the only Big Ten back to average more than 100 yards a game, running and passing. His

Posed pictures were common in the 1940s, including this one of George Taliaferro "carrying" the ball in 1945. The helmets were leather and there were no face masks. *Photo courtesy IU Archives.*

role as a star player at a major university enlarged his impact on African American boys beyond the confines of Gary, Indiana. William Wiggins would later, as an IU professor, describe Taliaferro's influence to writer Ryan Whirty: "Whenever guys played football in the backyard, everybody wanted to be George Taliaferro," he said. Professional football, which would further Taliaferro's influence, was in his future, but he still had a couple of years before it would significantly change his life. Although 1945 was a good football year for both Taliaferro and the NFL, each still had obstacles to overcome before their fates would become intertwined. Taliaferro had color barriers to fight, and a new professional football league, the All-America Football Conference, was about to challenge the dominance of the National Football League.

During the 1945 season, Taliaferro encountered racism on the football field and in Bloomington. But the racism that hit Taliaferro the hardest occurred right after the Big Ten championship. A wall-size picture of the 1945 championship team that ran as an ad in the Indiana University football game programs was hung on a wall at the Gables Restaurant, a restaurant on the "gown" side of Bloomington. "[The Gables] was just down the street from where Hoagy Carmichael wrote 'Stardust,'" Taliaferro said. Segregation prevented Taliaferro and the other black members of the football team from entering the popular restaurant, thus also preventing them from seeing the hand-tinted photograph which featured the 11 starters. Taliaferro was in the second row, just to the right of center. Occasionally, he would try to see the picture, managing to get just a glimpse. Since the picture hung on the far left wall, Taliaferro would go to the far right window of the Gables, cup his hands around his face and press his forehead against the glass. After several attempts turning his head this way and that, he discovered just the right angle to see some of the championship picture. He couldn't see the left side of the picture at all, no matter how he turned his head, but "I could see the most important person on that picture, which was me!" he joked. It would be another two years before Taliaferro actually had the opportunity to see the picture in its entirety.

In November, the Nuremberg Trials began. But while the trials truly meant the war was over, the draft was not. Before he had a chance to finish his freshman year, Taliaferro received a letter from Uncle Sam and was soon off to serve his country. He wouldn't be back to Indiana University in the fall to play for McMillin. Instead, like so many black servicemen, he would spend his time in the army fighting racism, a more visible enemy than any others he would experience as an American soldier.

The 1945 Hoosier Starting Eleven left to right: Ted Kluszewski, John Goldsberry, Richard Deranek, Howard Brown, Pete Pihos, John Cannady, George Taliaferro, Joe Sowinski, Ben Raimondi, Russell Deal, Bob Ravensberg. This hand-tinted picture hung in the Gables Restaurant to celebrate the undefeated season. Taliaferro didn't see the picture in its entirety until two years later since he was not permitted in the restaurant. *Photo courtesy IU Archives.*

GEORGE TALIAFERRO

20---GEORGE TALIAFERRO

Halfback — Indiana

Weight—195 lbs.   Age—20
Height—6'   Year—junior

Paced Indiana to 1945 Big Ten title with his running and passing. Gained 719 yards and completed 10 out of 19 pass-attempts. Voted all-Big Ten as freshman. Excellent broken field runner. Good pass receiver, too. Hails from Gary. Played under Bo McMillin, now coach of Detroit Lions.

ALL-STAR FOOTBALL GUM

Collect this series of Gridiron Greats.

Send 5 All Star Wrappers and 10c for big 12" x 6" felt pennant of any team listed on any All Star card.

N. Y. Giants	Navy
Michigan	No. Carolina
Stanford	Chicago Cards

Send Wrappers and Coin to
LEAF GUM CO., Box 5907 · CHICAGO 80, ILL.
Copyright 1948

A Leaf football card of George Taliaferro from 1945. Although it was his first season with Indiana University, he was a major contributor to the undefeated season and Big Ten championship.

Army Days

Although she had meant well, Mrs. Parham's advice, despite a rule that deferred state college students from the draft, ultimately had not kept Taliaferro from being drafted into the U.S. Army. In fact, his decision to attend Indiana University may have had the opposite effect, something he would only discover down the road. Later in life Taliaferro understood that being drafted led to significant events in his life that he wouldn't have changed. But when he received his draft notice on February 4, 1946, he was only aware that it meant he would be leaving Indiana and football behind. Shortly after he received his letter, he departed for his induction in Indianapolis and from there to Camp Atterbury in Edinburgh, Indiana, to be processed. That took only two days, and then it was time to leave again, this time for basic training. At Camp Lee army post in Petersburg, Virginia, Taliaferro would experience the basic training required of all soldiers, but unlike every soldier, his experience would also include dealing with racism and falling in love.

During basic, Taliaferro and the other new recruits were confined to the post for two months. During this time they received instruction in weapons, drills, and tactics, while enduring seemingly endless hours of physical training. While they were free to leave the post in the evenings and on weekends, they were required to report for roll call each morning. Under those circumstances, and having spent countless hours with each other in just a short period of time, the inductees quickly became acquainted. Among Taliaferro's fellow trainees were some University of Michigan football players, the same ones he had played against a few months before in IU's season opener. Conversations among them often consisted of their shared Big Ten football experiences. Often these conversations were just small talk, a way to pass time, in order to avoid the boredom that comes with the same daily routine. During one such exchange, however, Taliaferro made an interesting discovery. There

Despite the fact that World War II had already ended, Taliaferro was drafted after his freshman year into the army. He was stationed at Camp Lee in Petersburg, Virginia. Circa 1946. *Photo courtesy George Taliaferro.*

was a rumor, it seemed, that the political connections of one of the Michigan football coaches may have actually landed Taliaferro in the service. The Michigan players told Taliaferro that at the end of the season their coach had practically guaranteed the team that they would not have to worry about playing against freshman phenom George Taliaferro the following season. Taliaferro laughed at first thinking they were kidding, but the serious looks on their faces revealed that they weren't.

"Well, how could he know such a thing?" Taliaferro asked, still not quite believing what he was hearing. It didn't seem possible, especially since Mrs. Parham told him that attending IU could help keep him from getting drafted.

"All I can tell you is that's what he said," a Michigan player responded, not really offering any more in the way of explanation.

This information frustrated Taliaferro. In Gary, he was a star athlete in an integrated neighborhood. He was accepted for who he was, and he was seemingly in control of his life. In the last year, however, he had begun to experience racism and segregation. The idea that Michigan coach Fritz Crisler

During what should be his sophomore year at IU, Taliaferro plays for the Camp Lee army football team, seen here circa 1946. Taliaferro is in the front row, third from the left. *Photo courtesy George Taliaferro.*

could have that kind of an impact on his life solidified for Taliaferro the idea that he was no longer in control of it. The realization that so many others could affect what he could do settled like a heavy weight in his stomach. It was a lesson he would never forget.

Taliaferro could not confirm whether it was Crisler who had managed to get him drafted. However, it was true that the Michigan Wolverines would not have to play against him in 1946, and the 1946 Indiana and Michigan game had been anticipated as being a real duel between Michigan's halfback, Walt Teninga, and Indiana's George Taliaferro. Ironically, neither would end

up playing in the Big Ten in 1946. Teninga was in the same basic training at Camp Lee and was among those telling Taliaferro about the supposed "conspiracy" to keep him from playing Michigan. Not only was there no duel between Teninga and Taliaferro, two of the Big Ten's biggest talents, but they ended up teammates in the army—along with two other Michigan players, Al Wahl and George Chimes.

Taliaferro's contribution to IU's championship football team had not gone unnoticed by the U.S. Army, netting him a position on the football team and other advantages during his time in the service. For a soldier who had just completed basic training, Taliaferro was somewhat privileged. He was in the quartermaster division, the supply people for the military. Taliaferro,

Even as a soldier Taliaferro is noticed for his pigskin prowess. Circa 1946.
Photo courtesy George Taliaferro.

however, was put into the special services, a position which allowed him to choose his own assignment. He decided to do what he had done in high school; he played football, basketball, and baseball, and he trained boxers. These assignments, the result of his recognized athletic prowess, were designed to keep Taliaferro in the entertainment aspect of the service. They even kept him from going to Japan with the rest of his outfit. In fact, he never left the United States the entire sixteen months that he was in the service.

Taliaferro could not quell the racism that existed in every facet of his life, even when he was serving his country. Disadvantages, he was realizing, came with his skin color, no matter how exceptional his athletic skills. He wasn't the only one. On his army football team there were five other black football players, all, like him, serving their country in the U.S. military, and all experiencing the spoils of athleticism and the frustration of racism.

Taliaferro recalled one such incident. Stationed in Petersburg, Virginia, they had taken a couple of army buses to Aberdeen Proving Grounds in Maryland to play against another military installation's football team. It was not this particular game itself, but the return trip home, that was notable to Taliaferro. After the game Sam Francis, the head coach, made a last-minute decision to stay in Washington, D.C., for the weekend. He left Taliaferro, the team captain, in charge. Francis gave him some government vouchers and instructed him to use them on the way back to base to pay for the team's dinner at a restaurant. Having given those few instructions, Francis headed to D.C. and the team boarded the buses for Virginia.

They decided that as they were a Virginia-based group and since they wanted to wait until they were closer to base before they stopped, they would eat somewhere in Virginia. They drove through Maryland, and when they finally came upon a rustic restaurant in Alexandria, Virginia, they decided it was time to stop. By this time, they were already getting hungry. The entire football team climbed off the buses and walked into the restaurant, where they stood under chandeliers made of old wagon wheels. The place didn't look fancy, but as long as it had food they would be content. Taliaferro walked ahead of the others, government vouchers ready in his hand. Before he could say anything, however, the manager approached him.

"Hey! Hey! Hey! What are you doing? What are you doing?" the manager barked. He hadn't even reached them yet; he was shouting as he ran toward them, his arms pumping at his sides like he was running a race.

Taliaferro waited until the man was standing in front of him and began to explain. "Well, we are the football team from Camp Lee in Petersburg, Virginia, and we want to eat. We have a government voucher," he said, not understanding the intent behind the question.

The manager cut him off before he could finish. "You can't eat in here," he said abruptly. He didn't offer an explanation or an apology. That was it; it was simple.

"What do you mean we can't eat in here?" Taliaferro asked.

"*You* can't," the man said pointing directly at Taliaferro, the emphasis on the word providing Taliaferro all the explanation he needed. Suddenly it was clear to him exactly what the man meant.

"You mean because I'm colored?" Taliaferro asked him, trying to control his voice, but the waver in it indicating his growing resentment.

"That's right. *You* can't eat in here," the man said again, in the same tone, with the same emphasis on the word *you.*

Taliaferro was noticeably upset, but he did not want trouble, and he was getting used to being barred from places. He simply turned to his teammates and said, "Guys, let's go," signaling for them to leave.

Taliaferro and his black teammates turned and began to walk away.

Jerry Tuttle, a fullback from Ohio State, said: "George, you guys go ahead and get on the bus. We'll be right out."

Taliaferro shook his head okay. He didn't dwell on it; it had happened before. He and the other black members of the team would wait on the bus while their white teammates ate in the restaurant. They walked out to the buses while their white teammates remained inside.

They had only been waiting for several minutes when Tuttle, Teninga, and Tony Gator, a player from North Carolina, and the other white players came running out of the restaurant. They didn't stop until they were back on the bus.

"Let's go! Let's go! Let's go! And don't go down the main highway!" They shouted to the bus driver.

Puzzled, Taliaferro asked, "Well, what's the matter?"

"We just tore that place up!" Tuttle said.

"Oh my god, here we go. Now we're going to be court-martialed and shot before a firing squad," Taliaferro said.

He was more proud than worried though. He said of the whole experience, a big grin on his face, "Us Big Ten guys stuck together."

They may have gained some satisfaction from the impromptu "protest" in the restaurant, but their stomachs were less than satisfied. When they finally got back to Petersburg, Virginia, they were beyond hungry. Taliaferro thought of a place where they could all eat, where he had connections. Playing football for Indiana's championship team and All-American honors had earned him, he said, recognition even in the south. One such admirer owned a restaurant, The Green Lantern, in Petersburg. "It's on Halifax Street. I know we can eat there," Taliaferro assured his teammates. They drove to Halifax Street and found a place to park near the Green Lantern. Again, they all got off the buses and filed into the entrance of the restaurant.

This time when they entered, they were relieved to find that the greeting from the owner was a friendly one. "Hey, George!" he said, as he walked up to Taliaferro. There was a short pause as the man looked at the army football team in front of him. "Wait a minute, wait a minute. What are you doin'?" he asked, seemingly confused. Taliaferro again explained their situation. They were on their way back from a football game; their coach had stayed in D.C.

"and we have a voucher that we need to spend. We want to get something to eat," Taliaferro finished. It seemed simple enough.

The reply was unexpected. The owner was a fan of Taliaferro, had greeted them in a friendly manner, yet the man said, "You can't eat in here." It was the same sentence the white owner had pronounced earlier. Just like that. It really was simple enough.

"Come on. What do you mean?" Taliaferro asked, his frustration increasing with every minute the conversation continued, with every ridiculous explanation of a system that made no sense.

"Black people and white people can't eat in the same dining room in the state of Virginia," the man explained. It was a simple matter of the law. The army football team, which had been used to eating together on base, had been unaware of this.

Despite having repeatedly experienced the injustice of racism, Taliaferro was beyond belief. "Well in other words the guy in Alexandria was Jim Crow; so this is Joe Crow," he said, the hunger making it even harder to swallow the preposterous laws that kept him and his teammates from getting a meal.

That was the typical treatment that he and the other black servicemen received even though they were in the U.S. military. They were fighting for a country that didn't accept them, that saw them as second-class citizens, that sometimes acted as if they didn't exist. "Even being dressed properly in our uniforms did not make any difference," Taliaferro said. They left the Green Lantern, still hungry and with only one option left. They returned to base to eat in the mess tent, the only place the entire team was free to eat together, the unspent vouchers untouched in Taliaferro's pocket.

There was very little talking when they finally got to eat dinner. "We ate like butcher's hounds, we were so hungry," Taliaferro said. The short amount of time it took for him to eat his meal was the only time he wasn't thinking about what he had gone through that night to eat. As soon as his hunger was satisfied, he couldn't help but think about it more. His stomach was finally full, but Taliaferro felt cold and empty. It was disheartening to wear the uniform of the Army of the United States of America and to hear talk about defending the rights and freedoms of America, when he was not entitled to those rights and freedoms. He was in uniform to defend a country that did not want him, that treated him as if he were nothing. He wasn't the only black soldier to wrestle with that reality.

Segregated restaurants were only one small part of the racism Taliaferro encountered during his stint in the military. It was part of the experience of

Taliaferro with two of his Camp Lee teammates. On the far left is Mel Lewis of Howard University. On the right is Robert Alexander of UCLA. Circa 1946.
Photo courtesy George Taliaferro.

the black soldier, and he was no exception. Even though it was common, that did not mean Taliaferro had to accept it. There were times, like his dining experience, when he would just walk away, but sometimes it got to him so much that he couldn't keep it inside anymore. One of those times happened at an away football game. His team took a Greyhound bus from Petersburg, Virginia, to Fort Benning, Georgia, for one game. Once they had arrived at Fort Benning, Coach Francis was told that his black players could not stay in the same facility on the base with the white players. It was, after all, the segregated south.

During a phone conversation with his mother, Taliaferro had mentioned the Georgia game. Virnater Taliaferro was immediately worried. She did not want her son going to a southern state, where the racism was even more pronounced and often took a more violent, more physical form. She was so worried that she had even called Coach Francis to discuss the situation. She was worried that something would happen to her son in the racially charged state, she told him. Coach Francis managed to calm her down and quieted her fears. Her son, he explained, was in the U.S. military. He would have the full protection of the army behind him. He would see to that personally, he assured her. She still had her doubts, but she agreed to Taliaferro making the trip.

The full protection of the army, it seems, was no match for the Jim Crow laws of the south, laws that were embedded in the very culture. Once they arrived on base, Taliaferro and the other black members of his team were immediately segregated from the white players. They were sent to Sand Town, an area of the post where the black troops lived, while their white teammates were housed in a large brick dormitory. The brick barracks, unlike the simple wooden barracks of Sand Town, had standard amenities.

Even the food in Sand Town was of inferior quality. The meal prepared for them at breakfast was re-served to them for lunch. The eggs were hard and stuck stubbornly to the metal trays on which they were served. Taliaferro, who more often than not had ignored racism, simply refused to eat the food. He was too frustrated to overlook it this time. He called Coach Francis and told him that he and the other players needed some real food to eat. The leftover egg paste was not going to be sufficient. "And I have no intention of playing in that game tomorrow," he informed his coach, anger etched into every syllable.

In an act of solidarity, the other five black players also refused to eat the food or play in the game. Taliaferro, not wanting them to get in trouble, said, "Hey, you don't have to be a part of this. This happens to be the way that I feel and I feel this way because of the promise that Colonel Francis made to my mother indicating that I would not be discriminated against in any way, shape, form, or fashion, and since it has not happened, I am not in any way obligated to play the game." This was his fight; they did not have to stand with him, he said. His teammates felt the same way he did, though. Why should they play in the game if they were treated as inferior to the white players? They would continue to protest right alongside him. Their protests did not fall on deaf ears. Colonel Francis apparently had a chat with the commanding officer at Fort Benning, who then called for an audience with both Taliaferro and his coach.

Taliaferro walked into the room. Fort Benning's commanding officer, wasting no time, looked him in the eye and said, "Soldier, you can be dishonorably discharged."

Taliaferro would not be intimidated, though. He stood firm and answered, "Sir, I mean no disrespect, but you better start doing it, 'cause I won't play."

Until he and his black teammates were housed in the same barracks, given the same food, and treated with the same respect as their white teammates, Taliaferro continued, they simply refused to play in the game. It was a risk he had been willing to take, and it paid off. Opting not to pursue the dishonorable discharge, the commanding officer sent a weapons carrier, which resembles today's Humvee, large enough for all six of the black players. They got in with the little bit of baggage they had, and the weapons carrier took them back to the brick dormitory with the rest of the team. They would be playing in the game after all, a game that, according to the Sand Town cook, also signified change in Fort Benning, Georgia. Taliaferro had struck up a conversation with the man when he had first arrived in Sand Town. During a friendly exchange, the cook, a black man, had asked Taliaferro, "Whom are you going to play a football game against?"

"We are going to play the Doughboys," Taliaferro replied.

"No, you're not going to play the Doughboys," the cook corrected him, chuckling a little. "We have two football teams. We have a black football team and we have a white football team. And if you're going to play anybody, you are going to play the black football team."

"No, we are going to play the Doughboys," Taliaferro insisted. He hadn't realized Fort Benning had two teams, but he and his teammates had already been told they were competing against the Doughboys.

"I tell you what. I have two three-day passes in my pocket. I am going to give these passes away because I want to see you play the Doughboys in Fort Benning, Georgia. That's going to be history. It's going to be the first time that blacks and whites ever competed against each other in the state of Georgia," the cook said.

Taliaferro and his teammates did play the Doughboys, Fort Benning's aptly named all-white football team. A huge Georgia audience came to watch. The Doughboys, led by Captain John Green, a College Football Hall of Fame inductee, had a tremendous reputation. Five players from the United States Military Academy's 1945 national championship team were on that team. There was a huge OCS (officer training) attachment at Fort Benning, and many of the football players had been transferred there from West Point. The Doughboys were going to be a tough opponent.

The talent level and the weather made for a rough day. Taliaferro and many of his teammates, unaccustomed to the southern climate, had never played in temperatures that high before. They fought hard despite the weather, but so did the Doughboys. Both defenses were resolute, and the game remained scoreless for the first three-and-a-half quarters. The last eight min-

George Taliaferro runs the ball for his Camp Lee football team. Circa 1946.
Photo courtesy George Taliaferro.

utes of the game were a different story altogether, though. The Doughboys offense kicked in and scored several times in just eight short minutes for the win. They not only won, but dominated, winning the game 26 to 0. The Doughboys had capitalized on their dominant stamina in the southern heat. "I wondered if I almost had a heat stroke, and here it was October. But October in Georgia is still plenty hot," Taliaferro said. "We just got tired." But they had achieved a minor victory just by playing the Doughboys in Georgia and keeping them scoreless much of the game.

Being in the service was not all bad for Taliaferro, who was able to play the sports he loved. He was also about to meet the girl of his dreams, Viola Jones. Virginia State College for Negroes was located in Ettrick, Virginia. It was just outside of Petersburg, about five miles from Camp Lee, Taliaferro's base. On his first weekend pass, having nothing better to do, Taliaferro had an idea to pass some time. He rode the bus from Camp Lee to Petersburg, got directions in town, and walked to campus to watch the Virginia State Trojan football team in its spring workout. Upon finding the stadium, he climbed about halfway up the empty stands, and took a seat to watch, thinking about what he would be doing at Indiana University if he were there. McMillin was probably working on versions of the Cockeyed T with Taliaferro's teammates, he thought. Although he missed Indiana University, he knew he couldn't complain; he was fortunate just to have the opportunity to continue playing football while in the army.

Shortly after he arrived, another person climbed the same set of bleachers and sat near him. Taliaferro, lost in what was happening on the field, was unaware of the presence until the person asked, "Are you George Taliaferro?" Taliaferro, a little surprised that someone there would know him, affirmed that he was. The man introduced himself. "Milton Purvis," he said, and then explained that he had recognized Taliaferro by his civilian attire, which included the very colorful jacket given to members of the 1945 Indiana University team to commemorate its undefeated season and Big Ten championship.

Milton Purvis was the sports editor of the campus newspaper. He was familiar, he told Taliaferro, with his football success. Purvis also explained that there had been several articles written about the popular athlete coming to Fort Lee. The All-American, one article had indicated, would be seen in the area in the fall. So it hadn't taken Purvis long to identify him. The two men conversed for a while about football and the army, until Purvis excused himself and left the stands.

Taliaferro watched him go to the practice field where he talked to Virginia's Coach Jefferson for a moment, and realized they were talking about him when Purvis indicated toward the stands. Purvis motioned for Taliaferro to join them on the field, where Purvis made introductions. When Coach Jefferson asked him to tell the team about his experiences at Indiana and in the army, Taliaferro was taken aback at first. Many of the players on the team were older than Taliaferro. But when Jefferson gathered the coaches and team around, he had no choice but to do an impromptu speech. Despite his initial qualms, and the fact that he couldn't even remember what he said, he figured it must have been okay because when it ended he received both applause and expressions of gratitude. The Trojans resumed practice, and

Taliaferro accompanied Purvis back to the stands, relieved to be done with his speaking engagement.

The two men continued their conversation until practice was over. Though they had not known each other long, Purvis had been impressed by Taliaferro, and decided to introduce him to his "play sister." Historically, black colleges used a program of inviting freshman men and women to pair off as "play" brothers and sisters in order to have someone to whom they could relate and turn to as they adjusted to college life. Purvis invited Taliaferro to be his guest for dinner. Taliaferro accepted the invitation and followed Purvis from the stands. They talked all the way to the dining hall on campus, where they got in line, grabbed their trays, and decided on their food choices. With full tray in hand, Taliaferro walked behind Purvis who was scanning the dining room. Finding what he was looking for, he made his way to a table on the other side of the cafeteria. Three young women were sitting there, but Purvis was focused on one in particular. "George Taliaferro, I want you to meet my play sister, Viola Jones," he said. When he saw her, Taliaferro absolutely could not believe his eyes. The well-built beauty with dark hair that just brushed her shoulders had rendered him speechless. His mouth was open, but no sound came from his stunned lips. "The lights went out when Milton introduced us," he said of the encounter. Beyond that, he could not remember much of the meeting, just that he could not get over the beautiful Jones. "I was completely out of my mind and didn't want to make an ass out of myself," Taliaferro said. He was pretty sure they exchanged the usual small talk about hometowns, the army, college majors, and football, but that was the extent of it. Although he could tell that she was incredibly bright, she was not very talkative.

At the end of dinner, as they were saying goodbye, Taliaferro could only nod at the other two girls whose names would not come to him. And while he was relatively sure he had eaten because he had returned the empty tray to the wash area, he couldn't recall actually doing so. The only recollection he had of the entire meal was that he was so smitten by Viola Jones that everything else had left him. Once they had said goodbye to the girls, Taliaferro pumped Purvis for more information about her. He wanted to know more about the play brother/sister program and how long Purvis had been Viola's play brother. Purvis humored him. They had met as freshmen, he explained, and were on their third year as "siblings." He patiently explained how the program worked. But Purvis knew what Taliaferro was really getting at, so he came out and asked what Taliaferro was too shy to come out and say: "Do you want to see her again?" Taliaferro couldn't hide his eagerness. Of course he did. He hadn't been able to think of anything else since he had met her. Purvis told him where she lived and that he would find out what her dorm's visiting hours were so Taliaferro could see her again.

The idea that he would see her again was encouraging, but he still wanted to know more about the incredible young woman he had just met. Purvis graciously answered Taliaferro's questions. He told him that she worked as Coach Jefferson's secretary, that she was pursuing a degree in business education, and other things. Taliaferro did not want to leave campus that night, but eventually he had to go back to base. It was not long, though, before he had made plans for their first date. Dating off campus was not permitted for the Virginia State students, so his first date with Jones was spent on campus. The information from Purvis combined with his conversation with Jones herself was revealing. Beneath her quiet demeanor and modesty, she was actually one of the most popular girls on campus, he noticed. She was a cheerleader, a princess in the homecoming activities, and she was involved in several clubs. She also played tennis and volleyball and loved to dance. His first date had not been disappointing. He asked her out again, and many more dates followed, always on campus. They went to movies and concerts and out to eat. They even took in some football games. After a few weeks of dating, Taliaferro even brought a couple of his army buddies to meet the young woman he had been talking about. When it was time to introduce them, he was too nervous to remember her last name. Instead, he decided to introduce her as his girlfriend. He noticed happily that she hadn't denied it. She might have been trying to spare embarrassing him, he thought, or she might have agreed that their relationship was at a new level. Taliaferro preferred to believe the latter, and the fact that their dating continued into basketball season was a good sign. They took in some basketball games and even attended church together on occasion. They continued to go to the dances together and sometimes just strolled around campus talking. Taliaferro enjoyed her company, especially their conversations. As they learned more about each other with each date, Taliaferro began to wonder if maybe she was the woman with whom he would spend the rest of his life. He certainly hoped so.

As he walked to her dorm one afternoon, Taliaferro walked by a scale, the full-sized machines that tell one's weight and fortune. Shrugging his shoulders to indicate why not, he stopped and inserted a nickel. The arrow moved around the face of the scale, telling him that his weight was the same 195 pounds it had been for years. What was more significant was his fortune. He had told Bo McMillin he wasn't a superstitious person, but he had to wonder when he took the small card from the slot and read the words: *You will meet the campus queen.* Looking around to see if anyone else had witnessed the event and then realizing he was alone, he said aloud anyway, "I've already met her." Smiling, he couldn't help but wonder if just maybe the fortune was more than a coincidence. "It must be fate," he decided. It made him think again about his chance meeting with Milton Purvis that day in the football stadium and how Purvis had introduced him to the slim beauty who he now couldn't stomach leaving. Since that meeting, Taliaferro had spent all of his weekends on campus with her. Regrettably, school was closing for the summer, and Viola Jones was soon leaving to go back home. The thought of separating from her took the smile from his face, but he quickly made his way to her dorm.

He couldn't just let her go, especially if they were destined to be together. Taliaferro was prompted to take action. After only a couple of months of dating, he did the only thing he could think of to do. He simply asked her, out of the blue one day, "Will you marry me?" He could read no emotion on her face, not that he would have had the time. She did not hesitate.

Her response was a prompt and resounding, "No." The surprise in her voice was clear. She was only seventeen, she told him. She had graduated early from high school and had promptly enrolled in college. She had too many plans for her future. She wanted to graduate from college, get a job, and return home to help her parents financially. Even if that weren't the case, she continued, she really did not know him well enough. She didn't know enough about his background to marry him. She had plenty of reasons to justify her answer, but all Taliaferro heard was the no. He wasn't sure why he had expected her to say yes, but he had. He knew he was in love with her. Apparently, she just didn't feel the same way. Dejected, Taliaferro headed back to the post. Usually, he would arrive there in such high spirits after having spent time with the lovely Jones. This time he went straight to his bunk and took off all of his clothes. He walked into the latrine, stood in front of the full-length mirror, and asked aloud to no one, "How could she say no to perfection?"

At least her rejection had not completely ended the relationship. The two continued to correspond by mail over the summer. Taliaferro's position had not changed. He was still completely smitten by her. On a two-week furlough home to Gary, she was all he could think or talk about. He was miserably in love, and to make matters worse, his high school girlfriend was getting married, a painful reminder of his own rejection.

At the end of the summer, Taliaferro's furlough was over and Jones was headed back to school. Both returned to Virginia where they were able to continue their relationship where they had left off. Taliaferro hoped it would provide the opportunity for her to get to know him well enough to finally agree to marry him. They did continue dating; however, there was no more talk of marriage. Still, they enjoyed being around each other when the opportunity presented itself. They were both busy and Taliaferro, playing football for the post, was away at football games on alternate Saturdays. When they were together, he made his intentions to marry her clear, even though he never came right out and said it. He did not want to scare her off, and he did not want to be rejected again. Still, he wanted it to be clear how he felt. This seemed to be working. It seemed like he was finally making some progress in their relationship when she invited him, after the last football game on the Post, to visit her family in Evington, Virginia.

In Evington, he was introduced to her mother and father and her two brothers, both recently discharged from military service. Her father, a farmer and a practical joker, challenged the "city slicker" Taliaferro to strength, agility, and shooting contests, as well as other contests involving farming. Taliaferro wanted to make a good impression, but he was too competitive to just let her father win. The honest thing to do, he thought, was to try his hardest. The outcome was that he either equaled or beat her father in every contest. Viola's mother enjoyed that immensely and cheered Taliaferro on during the contests.

Apparently, Viola's father had seen enough, Taliaferro had apparently proven himself, and Mr. Jones suggested they all go inside for dinner. There was, of course, a large spread for dinner. They ate and talked about Taliaferro, his plans for football and college. The conversation continued after dinner as well. Taliaferro discussed the service, football, and other experiences late into the evening with Jones's brothers. Although Taliaferro did not drink, he accepted when her brothers invited him along to a local bar, where they visited with some of the other local men to catch up on the latest sports news. For Taliaferro, the family visit had been a huge success. Her family seemed to like him, and his relationship with the beautiful undergrad seemed to progress at a new level after the visit. She was introducing him to her background, something important to her. Taliaferro was hopeful that this meant she wanted to take the relationship further.

The couple continued seeing each other weekly until she graduated in June of 1947. Upon graduating, however, she took a job at the Tuskegee Institute in Alabama, home of World War II's first black fighter pilots, the successful Tuskegee Airmen whose 332nd Fighter Group never lost a bomber to enemy action. Like so many African Americans at this time, the Tuskegee Airmen fought both for their country and against the racism they experienced in it. Their fight against oppression in the U.S. Army Air Corps led the way to Executive Order #9981 desegregating the Armed Forces, which would be signed by President Truman in July of 1948.

Jones's move to Tuskegee meant a separation for the couple, but it would have happened soon anyway. Taliaferro didn't realize it, but he was soon getting discharged from the army. The couple managed to make the separation easier by corresponding through the mail, but it wasn't the same. He had grown accustomed to seeing her often and always looked forward to those times. Not seeing her was going to be difficult. There would be some compensation in the fact that he would soon be going to Gary, where he would have his family around to ease his loneliness.

Taliaferro couldn't be sure what happened, but he knew it started when he received a call from his Indiana University football coach Bo McMillin, who told him Frank Summers would be calling him. Summers was a fraternity brother of Taliaferro, but the two had never actually met. Taliaferro didn't know what the call would be about; he just knew to expect a call. Even when Summers did call, asking a series of questions and then requesting the name of a contact person, Taliaferro wasn't sure what was going on. He gave the information as requested, because McMillin had asked him to do so, but when he hung up the phone he was still unclear about what was going on. He dismissed it, assuming McMillin would explain eventually.

Within four days it became clear, though he hadn't heard from his former football coach. Taliaferro found out his outfit was to be shipped overseas to Japan as part of the post-war occupation. The day the group was to leave, however, Taliaferro was called by the first sergeant, the "top kick." The top kick was the guy who did everything for the administration. Taliaferro said, "If the commander wanted to communicate with you, in any way, they never lowered themselves to speak to you; the top kick did it all." Taliaferro went to see him, wondering what the top kick wanted. It was good news for Taliaferro who was handed two three-day passes and then told, "I'll see you when you get back." Taliaferro was confused; his outfit was leaving and he was being handed passes.

"Well, I didn't request anything," he said, fishing for information.

"Just go. You got six days. I'll see you when you get back," the top kick replied, not offering any more information than that, handing him the passes and dismissing him at the same time.

Taliaferro knew better than to argue, so he took the offered passes. Jones was no longer in Virginia, so he couldn't go see her. Instead, he decided to go to New Jersey to visit his Indiana University teammate Mel Groomes. He had planned on staying at the YMCA, but Groomes wouldn't allow it, so Taliaferro stayed with Groomes and the two spent time catching up. Groomes told Taliaferro about the 1946 football season, while Taliaferro told him about playing football for Camp Lee and about meeting Viola Jones. While the opportunity to visit was pleasant, it made Taliaferro homesick to hear about IU, and talking about Jones just reminded him that she was gone. After their visit, Taliaferro went back to base where he discovered that his outfit really had gone to Japan, leaving him behind. He was also told that he had been honorably discharged. His formal discharge was on June 23, 1947—16 months after he went into the army. Of his situation he said, "The same way they got me in, I got out. I didn't ask any questions."

A Volatile Time for Professional Football

While Taliaferro was in the service, professional football had continued to evolve. With the formation of the All-America Football Conference (the AAFC), the NFL was no longer going to have a monopoly on professional football. NFL commissioner Elmer Layden was so unhappy about the formation of the new league that he decided not to acknowledge its existence. The AAFC, however, described by Peterson as the "first serious challenge to the supremacy of the NFL," planned to begin sanctioning games in the 1946 season, whether Layden recognized it or not. The AAFC could not be ignored for long, and the subsequent feud between the two leagues made a lasting impact on the sport.

The new league had eight franchises, four teams in the East Division and four teams in the West Division. The East Division consisted of the New York Yankees, the Brooklyn Dodgers, the Buffalo Bisons, and the Miami Seahawks. In the West division were the Cleveland Browns, San Francisco 49ers, Los Angeles Dons, and Chicago Rockets. This new league was, in general, competition to the NFL. However, in three cities—New York, Chicago, and Los Angeles—the new league was in direct competition with established NFL teams, making the rivalry more fierce.

Because they would be vying for some of the same players and for some of the same fans, the AAFC's leaders wanted to have a preseason meeting with their NFL counterparts to discuss player contracts and territory rights. Still trying to ignore the new competitor, Commissioner Layden simply ignored the request to meet. According to an article in the *Chicago Daily Tribune,* Layden had said, "Tell them to get a football first." According to Peterson, Layden's curt reply was, "Let them get a football and play a game, and then maybe we'll have something to talk about." Interestingly, the AAFC's commissioner and president, Jim Crowley, and NFL commissioner Layden had both been a part of Notre Dame's legendary Four Horsemen.

Notre Dame's website tells the story of the famous quartet who earned their name in a game against Army when sportswriter Grantland Rice wrote: "Outlined against a blue, gray October sky the Four Horsemen rode again. In dramatic lore they are known as famine, pestilence, destruction, and death. These are only aliases. Their real names are: Stuhldreher, Miller, Crowley, and Layden." Harry Stuhldreher was the quarterback, Crowley was the left halfback, Don Miller the right halfback, and Layden the fullback. They were only sophomores, but they were running all over defenses under the leadership of Coach Knute Rockne. It was 1924, and Notre Dame was three games into a perfect season and eyeing a Rose Bowl championship when Rice coined the famous passage, which was then used by George Strickler, a Notre Dame publicity aide, to create the unforgettable image of the four men on horseback.

Despite their illustrious history Layden and Crowley, who would both eventually be elected to the National Football Foundation Hall of Fame, were no longer playing for the same side. Crowley responded to Layden's attempt to ignore the new league with a warning to the NFL. According to Peterson, Crowley said, "We originally resolved not to tamper with National League players, but since the NFL snubbed us we see no reason why we can't hire their players." The impact of this statement on professional football quickly became clear. The feud led to trouble for both leagues as they competed for players. The subsequent salary war inflated player compensation, which had financial ramifications for both the NFL and the AAFC.

Sportswriter Hugh Fullerton, Jr., noted that teams of both leagues reported losses because of the rivalry and the bidding up of player salaries in order to compete. Although inflated salaries were causing both leagues to suffer, the AAFC seemed to be winning the battle. According to Peterson, 44 of the 60 players on the 1946 All-Star team went to the AAFC. That small success wasn't enough to keep the AAFC out of financial difficulty, though. Edward Prell of the *Chicago Daily Tribune* wrote: "There has been a growing awareness of late that professional football's battle of dollars is taking its toll." Part of the problem, he explained, was the exorbitant player salaries. "Twenty-five years ago, the annual club salary perhaps was no more than $25,000. Now it is $250,000! A maximum of $175,000 would strike an average of $5,000 for the 35 players on a squad," he suggested. Both leagues were suffering, and it was soon very clear that both would be in trouble if something was not done to end the war between them.

Some thought the only way to resolve the issue was for the two leagues to merge. Prell, however, felt otherwise. To him, "there should be no swallowing up of one league by the other, for professional football then would revert to its dark ages—with lopsided schedules and the owner again holding too much of a whip hand over the player." Instead, he suggested following baseball's example by having 16 teams covering all metropolitan areas and ending the season with a final series between the two conferences. That wouldn't happen, however, until the two leagues began to communicate, and it didn't look like that would happen any time soon.

While the AAFC had difficulty initially, it managed to achieve minor success. Many key players were lured to the league and the franchises completed their schedules. Despite this, more and more money troubles were becoming evident for the AAFC teams. The Miami Seahawks were just one example. They had many unpaid bills for hotels and restaurants that they didn't have the funds to pay. Sparse home game crowds furthered their financial difficulties, and soon the league ended up having to pay the players' salaries for the Seahawks. By 1947 the league had taken back the troubled franchise. Luckily, a group of investors from Baltimore stepped in, and soon the Miami Seahawks had become the Baltimore Colts.

The changes in professional football were not affecting Taliaferro in 1946, but they would be significant to him in a couple of years. And although the war between the two leagues was important, of even greater interest to professional football was its re-integration. Unlike pro baseball, which had always been an exclusively white sport, black players had played professional football from its outset. The very first black professional football player was Charles W. Follis, who played from 1902 through 1906 with the Shelby Athletic Club. Robert W. Marshall, the second black professional football player, played for 20 years, from 1905 to 1925, for the Akron Indians. The list goes on. Other black players include Henry McDonald and Gideon Smith, who also played professional football in the early 1900s. McDonald played from 1911 to 1917 for the Rochester Jeffersons and "Charlie" Smith played one game for the Canton Bulldogs in 1915. Between 1920 and 1933 there were many more African American football players playing professionally. Frederick "Fritz" Pollard played for several teams between 1919 and 1925, Paul Robeson played from 1921 to 1922, and Sol Butler played from 1923 to 1926, to name just a few. Through 1932 there were at least 15 African Americans who either were playing or had played professional football. This all changed, however, in 1933. By then, professional football, like professional baseball, was an exclusively white sport.

Many factors shaped this color line. Peterson wrote that the same justifications for the color line in major league baseball also applied to professional football. The first justification was that many white ball players simply would not take the field with a black player. The fact that black players could not travel with the club because hotels and restaurants would not accommodate them was given as another justification. Training, which often took place in the south where it was illegal for blacks and whites to compete together, was another reason for the color line. Finally, the actual ability and mental capacity of the black players was questioned. They were simply not good enough or smart enough, according to some critics, to play professional football. To Taliaferro it is more likely that the same critics who said that blacks weren't good enough actually worried that black players would be better at the sport than their white counterparts. Either way, these justifications were used by both professional football and professional baseball to draw a color line in their respective sports.

Professional football added one more reason to the long list. Because football is a contact sport, there would be more opportunity for racism between players on the field. It was true that players did utilize the close contact for this purpose, and incidents of racism on the field were not uncommon. According to Peterson, Fritz Pollard, the first black star in the NFL said, "The white players were always trying to hurt me, and I had to be able to protect myself if I was going to stay in the game." Whether or not the justifications were true, there were other possible and more plausible reasons for professional football's color line. One such reason may have been Redskins owner George Preston Marshall. Peterson quotes historian Thomas G. Smith: "To avoid offending Marshall and southern players and fans, NFL owners may have tacitly agreed to shun black athletes. Marshall himself once publicly avowed that he would never employ minority athletes. Indeed, the Redskins were the last NFL team to desegregate, holding out until 1962." George Taliaferro had his own personal run-in with Marshall.

The Redskins, Peterson wrote, was the last team in the league to desegregate. The Redskins' first black football player, Bobby Mitchell, was not signed until 1962, long after the other teams had integrated. Signing Mitchell, even then, according to an article by Jeff Brown in *The Daily Mississippian*, was only because of pressure put on the Redskins by the federal government, which had indicated restricting the use of their new stadium if they did not integrate. Ironically, according to Brown, the Redskins had their most successful season in five years, just one year after finally integrating the team.

Football historians speculate that the economic impact of the Depression may initially have had something to do with the widespread discrimination in pro football. Peterson wrote that during the Depression, football teams had to cut from 33 players to a meager 22 in order to save money. (Today teams have 45 players because the positions have become so specialized.) The African American players were, of course, among the first to be cut. By 1932, Joe Lillard was the only black man still playing in the NFL. During this time, black players were forced to play for all-black professional teams or go to minor league teams instead.

Of the all-black pro teams, the most notable was the New York Brown Bombers. The Brown Bombers were coached by Frederick "Fritz" Pollard. Pollard had an interesting professional football career. He played for the Akron Indians in 1919. He went on to play for teams in the American Professional Football Association and in the NFL from 1920 to 1926. Pollard coached for some NFL teams as well—including Akron, Milwaukee, and Hammond—making him the first black coach in the NFL before the league managed to oust its African American players. Pollard and other black players experienced racism in the league even before the color lines were drawn. According to the Professional Football Researchers Association, for example, in 1926 the New York Giants were forbidden to take the field against the Canton Bulldogs until the African American quarterback for Canton voluntarily withdrew from the game. At that time, there were only five black players left in the NFL.

Of Pollard's all-black New York Brown Bombers, based in Harlem, there is very little information. This was, according to an article by professional football researcher John M. Carroll, because white papers did not cover the all-black team, and black papers, which generally came out on Thursday, would have been reporting on a game that had happened four days prior. While little is known, then, about the team, it is known that the Brown Bombers were one way Pollard had of fighting racism in the league. He put together a talented team to play against the league's all-white teams. The Brown Bombers began their career with five straight wins, and they did not lose until the final game of the season. Pollard organized the Brown Bombers, and later the Chicago Black Hawks, to fight the color line in the NFL. While Pollard made his point, that his black players were talented and deserved to play, he did not accomplish everything he set out to do. Some white teams, including both New York teams—the Dodgers and the Giants—refused to play Pollard's Bombers, and the Brown Bombers were struggling financially.

Still, Pollard's all-black teams were one option for African American football players during the 1930s and 1940s before professional football was re-integrated, and these teams continued opening doors for black players in the league. Another option for these players was the minor league teams. Of the minor leagues, the Pacific Coast Football League (PCFL) was more receptive to black players than the American Professional Football Association. In 1946, 13 years after the color ban in the NFL, two of the Pacific Coast Football League's players integrated the NFL. Kenny Washington, the first black player in the league since 1933, and Woody Strode were both signed by the Los Angeles Rams that year, finally re-integrating the league. The Los Angeles Rams were formerly the Cleveland Rams, but the team had relocated to Los Angeles in 1945. Washington and Strode had Los Angeles connections as well. Both men attended UCLA at the same time as baseball's Jackie Robinson, and both, like Robinson, had been very popular college athletes. It wasn't until they were in their thirties, however, that they ended up with the Rams.

Later in that 1946 season, two other black men, Marion Motley and Bill Willis, also crossed the color line into professional football by playing for the Cleveland Browns of the All-America Football Conference. Motley and Willis, both eventual Professional Football Hall-of-Famers, constantly encountered racism on the field. According to Peterson, players would purposely step on Motley's hands with their cleats on, even when a play had ended. In one game, Peterson wrote, referee Tommy Hughitt finally managed to put an end to it. Noticing what was going on, he began penalizing these teams fifteen yards each time the incident occurred. Other referees took note and they, too, started to protect the league's black players from this blatant racism.

Motley, according to Peterson, said: "Of course, the opposing players called us nigger and all kinds of names like that. That went on for about two or three years, until they found out that Willis and I was ball players. Then they stopped that shit. They found out that while they were calling us names, I was running by 'em and Willis was knocking the shit out of them. So they stopped calling us names and started trying to catch up with us."

Willis and Motley also had Jim Crow laws with which to contend. While the Fourteenth Amendment prohibited state governments from racial discrimination, it did not restrict private organizations or people from doing so. Therefore, businesses like restaurants, hotels, and even movie theaters could discriminate, and the system of segregation became widespread. This system of segregation carried over to professional football. When the Browns played Miami, for example, Willis and Motley stayed home in Cleveland. While it was widely accepted, not everyone agreed with the south's system of segregation. According to Peterson, a Cleveland columnist wrote after the

Miami game, "It seems that a majority of the law-makers down in Florida don't know yet that the Civil War is over."

Black players like Washington, Strode, Motley, and Willis were a promising sign, but segregation still dominated professional football. The Los Angeles Rams was the only NFL team in 1946 with black players. By this time, Taliaferro had finished his military service and returned to Indiana. He, like Willis and Motley, was also experiencing racism and segregation. He, like Willis and Motley, was also going to make professional football history, and more important, strides against racism—in just a couple of years. First, though, he had to go back to Indiana University, where he still had a couple of years of college football to play.

Back at Indiana University

Taliaferro no longer lived at the Mays home when he returned to Indiana University in the summer of 1947. It was the summer that Jackie Robinson broke major league baseball's color barrier, despite taunting by players and fans, by starting at first base for the Dodgers. Robinson fought through discrimination all season to earn Rookie of the Year honors in the National League. He went on to play for ten years, helping the Dodgers to six pennants and a World Series championship. Robinson, like Taliaferro, was breaking down racial barriers, but society was slow to change.

When Taliaferro returned to Indiana University, he still was not permitted to live on campus, so he got a job cleaning the office of a female pediatrician in town and rented a room in a small building attached to the back of the office. This was a novel idea for the time, and other black students wanted to know how Taliaferro had managed to get a room to himself. At the Mays home, they were still packed in with three or four people to each small room. Little had changed on the campus while Taliaferro was in the army. Upon his return he planned to finish his HPER (Health, Physical Education, and Recreation) degree and prepare for the 1947 football season. He also continued to write and phone Viola Jones. Taliaferro found that despite not playing for Indiana in 1946, his return was met with a warm welcome. Taliaferro was still earning respect on the football field.

His prominence as an athlete aside, he still had to cut across campus to go to the Mays' home to eat because places like the Gables Restaurant and the Book Nook on campus still did not permit African American customers. Taliaferro finally reached a point where he could no longer accept this outright racism. Maybe it was having fought through some of the segregation he experienced while in the army. Or maybe it was that he had regained some of his former confidence. Whatever the reason, in a complete state of frustration and anger, Taliaferro decided it was time to see Indiana University president Herman Wells about the segregated restaurants on IU's campus. He couldn't ignore them anymore. He didn't realize what a strong ally he would have in Wells.

"Describe Santa Claus and you got Herman Wells," Taliaferro said of the man whose term as president of the university was marked by his focus on integrating the campus and on the controversial Kinsey Report. The Kinsey Report came out a few years after Taliaferro left Indiana, but he had been a participant. Kinsey, he said, was "some kind of a human being." Of Wells's ability to justify the study to a conservative public, Taliaferro explained, "He handled it with the aplomb of a magician." Wells had managed to convince many doubters that Indiana was assertive at researching every area of human behavior and that Kinsey's research on sexual behavior was an important aspect of that whole picture.

His personality may have helped. Like Santa, Wells was always jolly; he even tried to get to know all of the students. He would walk the campus every day at lunch to meet as many of his 10,000 students as he could. It was Wells's focus on the students and his commitment to integrating the campus to which Taliaferro appealed. To Wells he explained how he was not permitted in the restaurants on campus (many on the town side were also off limits to him) because of his skin color. Due to his class schedule, this caused problems for him every single day. He did not have time to run to the Mays' home and back to campus in the short amount of time he was allotted between classes, he explained. On the other hand, he could not eat at the restaurants that were right next to his classes. "I have a dollar and 25 cents in my pocket, and I have to go all the way to Mr. and Mrs. Mays's house to eat," he told Wells, trying to control his voice, but his face showing his frustration. Taliaferro explained that there were some restaurants on Kirkwood Avenue that were on campus and would provide him the opportunity to eat and get back to class, were he permitted to enter those restaurants. One was the Gables Restaurant, on whose wall the 1945 Big Ten Championship football team picture still hung. Taliaferro had yet to see it in its entirety.

Wells listened attentively while Taliaferro told his story. Then he took action, typical of Wells, the man who had convinced J. C. Coffee to integrate the pool simply by jumping into it. Taliaferro hadn't been sure how Wells would react to his plea for help; he just knew that he had to try something. Now he had his answer. Wells picked up the phone and called the Gables owner Pete Poolitsan. Upon exchanging greetings with the man, Wells asked him very bluntly if "Negro" students were permitted to eat at his restaurant.

Poolitsan explained that he couldn't permit it. African American students in his restaurant, he explained, might deter white students from eating there, thus causing him to lose the majority of his business. Apparently, Wells was less than sympathetic.

Taliaferro hasn't forgotten Wells's response to Poolitsan. In appealing to the man's business sense, Wells said, "Well, maybe I'll have to make all of the restaurants on Kirkwood off limits to ALL of the students." Losing Indiana University students would mean certain failure for the restaurants. Wells had Poolitsan right where he wanted him, and suddenly he was more than willing to make a deal. An agreement was reached that Taliaferro could eat at the restaurant for one week with an African American friend of his choosing. If there were no complaints after the one week, Taliaferro and his friend could bring two more friends and eat there for another week. If there were no complaints after the second week, Poolitsan would permanently allow African Americans to visit his establishment.

Taliaferro and his teammate Mel Groomes, who still lived at the Mays' home, ate lunch at the restaurant for one week. This was Taliaferro's opportunity to finally see in its entirety the 1945 championship picture that had been hanging inside the Gables for the past two years. That was the first thing he and Groomes did upon entering the restaurant—look at that picture. For a while, Taliaferro couldn't stop staring at it. Eventually the two sat down to lunch, hearing no complaints from other visitors to the restaurant. This continued for the week, and every time they walked in, they looked again at the picture. At the end of the week, when there were no complaints about their presence in the restaurant, Groomes and Taliaferro made arrangements to take dates the following week and see what the response was to that. Taliaferro's date was Betty Guess, a friend who later ended up marrying Bill Garrett, the Indiana University basketball player who would integrate Big Ten basketball in 1948. Of course, Taliaferro and Groomes pointed out the 1945 championship picture to the women. This time, the four of them sat down to eat, again meeting no resistance or disagreement from the other visitors. Even a poll taken on campus about the "experiment" supported the integration of restaurants. President Wells had helped Taliaferro, Groomes, and their dates successfully integrate the Gables Restaurant. The Book Nook, which was just a couple of doors down, soon followed suit.

This was just one of President Wells's attempts to desegregate the campus. According to a Wells biography, Wells would later receive the NAACP (National Association for the Advancement of Colored People) Brotherhood Award for 1961–1962 for such attempts as these. It was Wells who successfully desegregated the Union building on campus by simply having the placards which read "colored" removed from the tables there. His effect on the Bloomington campus was evident in the citation for the award, which read in part: "Both Indiana University and Bloomington are far better places, in terms of race relations, than they were a quarter-century ago." Taliaferro's experience with Wells was one of the many attempts the president made during his tenure to eliminate discrimination on the Indiana University campus.

After helping to integrate the restaurants, Taliaferro decided there was more he could do. The movie theaters were next, but not at his suggestion. One of the most popular pastimes for Indiana students, the theaters were also among the most obvious in their discrimination. The movie theaters' "colored" patrons were only permitted on Fridays, Saturdays, and Sundays, and then only in the upstairs seating. When Taliaferro was approached by the manager to help integrate the Indiana Theater, which stood just around the corner from the Gables, he was happy to do so. The plan, similar to the way Wells and Coffee had integrated the pool and he had integrated the restaurants, was to rely on Taliaferro's status as an athlete. The manager wanted Taliaferro to come to the theater any weekday, a day "colored" people weren't normally permitted, and sit in the typically off-limits downstairs section. It was presumed that his popularity on campus would prompt acceptance of his presence in the whites-only section of the theater. Just as it had at the Gables, the plan worked. Ironically, it was as if no one even noticed. Soon other African American students followed his lead and sat in the whites-only section. To the manager's delight, there were no complaints.

Taliaferro's successes prompted him to do more. At the Princess Movie Theater down the street from the Indiana Theater, he used a screwdriver to take down a large "Colored" sign, and then he again sat in the whites-only section, achieving the same result as he had at the Indiana Theater. He was again joined by some of his peers. Taliaferro, who still has that sign, and others who were brave enough to challenge the status quo, managed to quickly and quietly integrate Bloomington's movie theaters. As the first black student teacher from IU at University High School, Taliaferro continued to use his influence to make gains in race relations in Bloomington. The fact that he did not face resistance to the changes he was making may suggest Bloomington was a town ready for change.

While he was busy making important social changes, Taliaferro was also continuing his football success, and this was to be the year of "The Run." In the 1947 Dad's Day game against Pittsburgh, Taliaferro ran for a play neither the Pittsburgh nor the Indiana spectators will ever forget. In an *Indiana Dai-*

ly *Student* article, David Hackett wrote: "It is simply called The Run. To those who saw it, no other explanation is needed; it may be the most exciting play in IU football history." If one looks only at the numbers, The Run is actually not all that impressive. Starting at the 50 and ending at the 11, it was actually a gain of only 39 yards, a decent gain, but not something utterly memorable just for the distance. "I sure felt like I ran a mile though," Taliaferro was quoted as saying in the article. And that is why The Run was so remarkable: it still prompts discussion from Indiana football fans today, decades after it happened. Hackett described why it was so impressive: "Taliaferro zig-zagged from sideline to sideline, breaking twelve tackles in all. Every Pittsburgh player hit him but failed to bring him down. One poor fellow failed twice. Finally, he was gang-tackled at the eleven." Taliaferro was never able to see his famous run. In a Hammel article years later Taliaferro explained why: "They filmed the games then, but it happened that the Indiana photographer ran out of film just before that punt. He was changing his film." Taliaferro checked, but Pitt didn't have the film in their files either. He wondered if maybe that was better. "If I had seen it, I don't know if it would have had the mystique to me. It's funny, but I never go into the stadium that my mind isn't drawn to the spot where it started: on the north sidelines at the 45," he said.

After the game, Taliaferro ran through the gauntlet, a line of fans waiting to congratulate the players. "They slapped me on the back saying, 'How great thou art,'" Taliaferro said. The gauntlet was so long it took Taliaferro from the stadium to the Mays' house, where a number of black players and their families were having a reception. There, Taliaferro's father was waiting for him. Although he didn't understand football and had been to only a couple of his son's games, he had taken a train from Gary to attend the Dad's Day game and watch his son play. At the reception, Taliaferro heard a man ask Robert Taliaferro, "Is your son on the football team?" With a fat cigar hanging from his mouth, Mr. Taliaferro pointed to his son, took the cigar out, and said, "That's my boy." To Taliaferro, who was accustomed to being written about in articles and running the gauntlet of adoring fans, it was the best compliment he had ever been paid. Those three words hit him harder than any others ever had. "Because my dad owned me," Taliaferro explained. It wouldn't be long before he would think back on those words and cherish them as a treasured memory of his father. The satisfaction he felt that moment he wouldn't feel again until later in life when each of his four daughters would also "own" him in some way. Each one at some point would say, "That's my dad" and point to him with the same pride that his dad had shown when he acknowledged him after that game.

George Taliaferro and Mel Groomes walk with Hoosier fans after the game against Pittsburgh on October 18, 1947. *Photo courtesy IU Archives.*

With the exception of The Run and his father's pride, the 1947 football season was not as successful as that first, undefeated season Taliaferro played for the Hoosiers. The Hoosiers ended the season with a 5-3-1 record, tying for sixth place in the Big Ten Conference. The team had at least eked out a win over archrival Purdue, 16 to 14, which allowed them to retain custody of the Old Oaken Bucket. The Battle of the Bands made a return in 1947, but in a slightly different format. This time the battle was held in the University Men's Gymnasium at IU, with two bandstands at either end, during Sigma Delta Chi's Annual Blanket Hop. The fraternity gave out "I" blankets to outstanding graduating senior athletes at the dance. Taliaferro was not yet a senior, so he did not receive a blanket, but he was still receiving plenty of recognition.

He was named second-team All-American again in 1947. He had rushed 339 yards, averaging almost four yards a carry. He scored four touchdowns and punted an average of 35 yards per kick. The honors didn't end there. In

December Taliaferro was also named one of 65 outstanding college football players. He was invited to a weekend and dinner at the Waldorf Astoria hotel in New York City. The event provided Taliaferro with the opportunity to reconnect with Viola Jones, who had agreed to be his date for the evening. She had two brothers and two sisters in the city; she decided that she could visit them while she was in New York. She planned to stay with her sister Anna, even though she already had a room reserved at the hotel.

Taliaferro and Jones, along with four football players from other schools and their dates, attended the ball at the Waldorf together. Although she wasn't the campus queen any longer, Jones still loved to dance and was on the floor for every tune, her vitality reminding Taliaferro why he had fallen in love with her in the first place. She managed to wear him out on the dance floor, and he worked up a strong appetite. He sat out a dance in order to find food, and his friend Earl Banks decided to join him. The ladies kept dancing. Taliaferro and Banks found something to eat and sat down at a table only to discover they were surrounded by forks. Neither of them was sure exactly which fork it was that they should use for their salad. In fact, they couldn't even make out which forks belonged to which setting. They talked it over and, because they were both right handed, Taliaferro finally said they should eat with the forks to their right. Having reached that conclusion, they shrugged, picked up their respective forks and dug into their salad.

Taliaferro's lack of proper table etiquette was discovered when Jones and the others returned to the table. One of the other women took one look at the two men eating their salad and declared that they had used the wrong forks. As it so happened, Taliaferro was eating his salad with her fork. She informed him, rather snootily, he thought, that etiquette required him to use the fork on the left, not right. Jones tried to smooth things over by offering one of her own forks to the young woman, who seemed unrelenting in her campaign to embarrass Banks and Taliaferro. Her refusal to accept a fork from Jones had taken the last of Taliaferro's patience. He said, "I am right handed. I am eating my salad with this fork, and she better accept Vi's offer or she will have to go without a salad." The fork issue was resolved quickly after that, but the episode proved to be a valuable lesson for a man who would be attending many more important dinners over the years.

The experience at the Waldorf was further proof for Taliaferro of what an amazing woman Jones was. He had known it before but was even more convinced of it after. Jones was someone with whom he could see himself spending the rest of his life. After the ball that night, Jones stayed at the Waldorf Astoria with him. Even so, the weekend seemed short to Taliaferro, who once again had to say goodbye to the beautiful, classy woman who had won his heart. Jones returned to Alabama, and Taliaferro returned to Bloomington.

Although there was much to celebrate—his relationship with Jones and the fact that he was still tearing up the football field—1947 turned out to be a bad year for Taliaferro. He returned to Gary over the Christmas holiday to visit his family, something he had been looking forward to doing. On Christmas Eve he gave his parents a present and then told them he would see them early the next morning. They were going to a Christmas party with neighbors, the DeMents, and he was going to a party with an old high school friend, Adam McCullough. McCullough was playing football for Wilberforce University, one of the universities that had been recruiting Taliaferro just a couple of years earlier. McCullough and his girlfriend wanted to introduce Taliaferro to a girl who was a friend of theirs. Although he wasn't interested in her, he was a twenty-year-old college student, so he was interested in going to the party to hang out with friends. Taliaferro and McCullough went to East Chicago, near Gary and still in "the region," to McCullough's girlfriend's house. They weren't there for very long before Taliaferro felt an urgency to leave. He told his friend, "I have to go home." He didn't know why; he just had a feeling that there was an emergency. Something told him that he had to get home right away.

When he arrived at his house, his mother and the DeMents were walking out the front door and getting into a car. "You're celebrating Christmas really early," he joked with them. Knowing they would have just returned from a party, he asked, "Where are you going now?" The same feeling that had made him come home early was still tugging at him, but he tried to maintain a sense of normalcy. Something was not right and he knew it, but he wasn't ready to hear whatever his mother was going to tell him.

"We're going to the hospital," she answered, ignoring his attempt at joking. Her tone brought that tugging feeling to the surface. Then he heard the rest of her sentence and a heavy wall came down. Everything he heard and saw after that was muffled, as if from the end of a dark tunnel or under water. It couldn't be real. His mother and the DeMents were going to the hospital because his father had been shot. He knew, without being told, exactly when it had happened; it was the same time he had felt the sudden and overwhelming urge to get home from the party.

Taliaferro's Uncle Walter had been at the Christmas party with his parents. When they left the party, they stopped by Walter's apartment to visit for a little while. The two men were looking at a shotgun, a present Walter had received for Christmas. Robert Taliaferro walked out onto the balcony examining the gun. A hunter, he had to aim at something to get a feel for the gun, so he pointed it up at the stars. Apparently satisfied with what he saw, he then walked back into the apartment nodding his approval. Uncle Walter wanted to point out one more feature. "Let me show you something," he said. Taliaferro's father turned the butt of the gun to his brother to hand it to him, but as they made the exchange, it went off, blowing away much of the left side of Robert Taliaferro's body. The two men hadn't realized the powerful shotgun was loaded.

Seconds felt like hours as Taliaferro accompanied his mother to the hospital. When the DeMents finally pulled the car up to the entrance, Taliaferro wasted no time jumping from his seat and running inside. Even though it was early in the morning, someone was manning the information desk. He frantically asked for his father's room number.

"Room 203," she said, and before she could give further direction he was gone.

He moved quickly to the second floor and located his father's room. It was dark when he pushed open the door, the only light coming from the dimly lit hallway. Even though there was no way his father, whose bed was around the corner, could see him, Taliaferro heard him ask, "Junior?" Taliaferro had a younger brother who shared his father's name, but the nickname "Junior" had always been his alone. His father knew he was standing there. In the mere seconds it took Taliaferro to round the corner and get to the bed, however, his father had died. His last word was the question, "Junior?" That his father had seemed to understand he was there was only minor comfort. He hadn't been able to say goodbye, and it was Christmas morning.

The untimely death of Robert Taliaferro, who was only forty-two years old, sent his loved ones reeling. The man Taliaferro described as a "quiet disciplinarian," was small by most standards at 5'7" and 155 pounds. Not small, however, was the impact he had made on his son. During his childhood, Taliaferro had always thought that to be like his father would be "the greatest thing that could happen to a person." Despite having just a fourth-grade education, Robert Taliaferro was an intelligent man who could talk shrewdly about any subject and accomplish any manual task. The only thing Robert Taliaferro could not do was work with electricity. He just didn't understand it, Taliaferro said. But he did everything else, including carpentry, masonry, and plumbing. He also had a keen sense of what was important, and had managed to instill in his son a set of values that would carry him through life, including the importance of education, honesty, and a strong work ethic.

Had he not offered his son the choice of quitting and supporting himself or staying in school and being allowed to remain at home, Taliaferro would have quit high school in order to work in the steel mill like his father. Instead, his father's tough love kept him in school, where his football ability led to a college education and the possibility of a better way of life. Two years after his near withdrawal from high school, when he was leaving for his first semester at Indiana University, his dad had pulled out his worn, brown wallet and laid out a five-dollar bill and five ones, all the money he had in the world. He told Taliaferro he was going to split it with him because he was proud of him for finishing high school and for going to college on a scholarship. He asked which half Taliaferro wanted. Taliaferro remembered saying, "I'll take the ones. It'll look like I have more money that way." Then he told his dad he would never ask him for anything again. He didn't want to have to ask. Not because his father wouldn't give him help, but because it was such a struggle for him to do so. Taliaferro remembered standing in line for eggs and powdered milk to keep enough food on the table. The food-relief lines, Taliaferro said, were part of President Roosevelt's New Deal. Families were able to get a certain amount of free food based on the number of people in the family. His father, too proud to accept food he didn't work for, refused to go. His mother, however, said, "My children are going to eat," and went anyway. Taliaferro did keep his word, and he never asked his father for anything. Nevertheless, his life was certainly going to change without him.

Taliaferro couldn't quite escape the torrent of emotions that came with his father's unexpected death. There was a grief so intense it seemed to weigh down every cell of his body. And there was a tremendous sense of worry. His mother, he knew, would be struggling both financially and emotionally now. He wanted to leave Indiana University in order to get a job to help her. He remembered promising her as a young boy that he would take care of her someday. He didn't want her to become a maid and leave her own home in order to take care of someone else's, especially when she still had children at home who needed her. Giving up a college education and football would have been a sacrifice he would have made for her without hesitation, except for one thing. He had also promised both his mother and father that he would get a college degree, and his mother would not want him to give that up. He decided to finish out the school year and make his decision over the summer.

When the school year ended Taliaferro went to work in the same steel mill where his father had worked. In fact, he was in the "Tin Mill," his father's section, working with the same group of men for whom his father had been a supervisor. The first day he couldn't help but think that he was in the same place his father had so often been, and it was a painful reminder of his loss. Soon, however, rather than sadness, the job brought a sense of comfort to Taliaferro, who felt closer to his father while working there. Not only that, but it also helped Taliaferro work through the internal conflict that had plagued him for months. He mentioned to the crew his thoughts about quitting school to work at the mill permanently in order to help his family. They didn't hesitate to give their opinion, but the response he received was unexpected. These men had worked for Robert Taliaferro and knew him well. They knew without question that he had wanted Taliaferro to get a college degree. Moreover, he absolutely did not want his son to have to work in the steel mill his entire life like they all had. It was a hard life that was difficult to escape. When they reminded him of his father's wishes, it was as if he were there telling him in person, and Taliaferro knew that he had to go back to IU.

His mind finally set, he headed back to Bloomington at the end of that summer. He was comfortable with his decision at first, confident that it had been his father's wish. His mother's well-being, however, continued to haunt him. He had promised his father he would get an education, true, but he had also promised that he would take care of his mother if anything ever happened. He simply could not keep both promises. He knew if he stayed in school, he wouldn't stop thinking about his mother back in Gary, struggling to take care of the house, the kids, and herself. He just wasn't sure she could do it on her own. He returned to campus in 1948 still uncertain about his future there.

Taliaferro was in for more disappointment. This was also the year that he would lose another important mentor. Bo McMillin resigned from his coaching position at Indiana to be the head coach and general manager for the Detroit Lions. Although coaching professionally was a good opportunity for McMillin, it was obvious during a farewell banquet held in his honor that McMillin felt strong ties to Indiana University. According to an *Indiana Daily Student* article, McMillin said during his farewell speech: "I never could repay Indiana in 50 years for what it's done for me in 14 years." Then, crying, he hugged Vern Huffman, the All-American whose jersey number Taliaferro had inherited. McMillin's abrupt departure was difficult for Taliaferro, especially on the heels of his father's death, and he became something of a recluse. Having lost two of the most important men in his life, Taliaferro felt lost and alone.

That changed upon meeting Clyde Smith, Bo McMillin's replacement. Despite having just met him, Smith was such a kind person that Taliaferro couldn't help but come out of his shell. Like McMillin, Clyde Smith was a fairly small man at 5'7". Since Smith had been a line coach under McMillin, he was familiar with the way McMillin had run the program. While this helped to some extent, it was obvious that Smith would have his work cut out for him. Getting the program going and playing one of the toughest schedules in the NCAA would present numerous challenges, especially since the majority of the starters from the 1945 season were gone. All-American Pete Pihos was coming back during spring training as an assistant coach under Clyde Smith, but it was going to be a difficult year of transition for the Cream and Crimson.

Football kept Taliaferro busy for the first few months of the school year, but it didn't keep him from worrying. He understood that his parents didn't want him to end up in the steel mill, but there was another way he could help. Playing professional football would allow him to ease his mother's financial burden. He began considering it seriously, but at first didn't tell anyone. He had to be sure it was what he needed to do. When he answered letters from Jones, which were the only bright spots of those dark days, he didn't tell her of his desire to quit school to go pro. The situation was hard enough to explain to his mother, let alone to the woman he wanted to spend the rest of his life with. Jones, in the meantime, had taken a job at Howard University in Washington, D.C., as an assistant to the dean of the medical school.

With his older brother, who had a family of his own, in the Navy, Taliaferro felt that the responsibility to take care of his mother and younger siblings rested solely with him. His struggle with the decision ultimately changed the course of events in his life. Like his father, his mother's education was limited, and although she was an intelligent woman, she had only a sixth-grade education. She had worked, like so many women, during World War II making ammunition, but for the most part, she had stayed at home to raise her family. Now, without her husband, she was struggling to make ends meet.

Taliaferro pondered his situation, eventually sharing his concerns with the athletic director who, in turn, urged him to speak to President Wells. Wells couldn't make the decision for him, but did reassure Taliaferro that he would be there for him regardless of his decision. "Do whatever you have to do," he told Taliaferro. He did know what he had to do, but convincing his mother would be no small task. She would just have to accept it, he thought.

Herman B Wells and his mother, Anna Bernice Harting Wells, attend the October 16, 1948, homecoming game against Ohio State. Like McMillin, Wells was ahead of his time in race relations and fought to desegregate Indiana University's campus. *Photo courtesy IU Archives.*

He was going to convince her once and for all that he should quit school. This was easier said than done, because she was adamant that he stay in school. She knew about his friend Buddy Young, who had quit the University of Illinois his sophomore year and had not returned to get his degree. She thought that once you quit, once you broke ties with the university, you were done and could not go back. It was not until after the 1948 game against Purdue that Taliaferro began to convince her otherwise. Virnater Taliaferro traveled to West Lafayette, Indiana, with Taliaferro's aunt to watch the game against archrival Purdue. The game was a brutal one, and at the end, Taliaferro was carried off the field on a stretcher.

"I was not hurt," he said, "Just tired—because I was the only person on that team Purdue had to worry about carrying the ball—and they buried me in the ground." Indiana had been shut out. Purdue beat them 39 to 0, making up for some of the humiliation Indiana had handed them in recent years, and Taliaferro felt the beating personally, in every muscle in his body. After he recovered enough from his fatigue, he tried once more to talk to his mother about his idea of playing professional football. He indicated his exhaustion and pointed out his battle wounds to her. "The difference between getting pummeled on the field in college," he explained to her, "versus getting pummeled on the field in professional football . . . is that I'd get paid." "I could also take care of you, Claude, and Ernestine," he added.

She was not entirely convinced. "Remember your promise to your father," she reminded him. It was something he did not need to be reminded of at all, although numerous people had reminded him of it, including himself, since his father's death. It was something he had been struggling with for almost a year. Taliaferro had finally come up with a solution to his problem, a way to fulfill both promises—to take care of his mother and to get a college degree. He answered, "Mom, I will get it. I will have it put into my professional contract that I must return to Indiana University to get my degree." So, he informed her, he actually could play professional football and still receive an education. He wouldn't be breaking ties with the university at all. With that, his mother was convinced.

Just bettering the previous year's record, the Hoosiers tied for fifth place in the Big Ten Conference in 1948. There were simply too many forces working against them. Still, it was disappointing for Hoosier fans, who had felt the elation of that spectacular 1945 season. Clyde Smith was able to get his boys off to a strong start with two consecutive wins to start the season, but they could not hold on to the momentum. Taliaferro had a solid season though, lettering again and bettering his previous season's record in punting with an average of 41 yards. He rushed for 262 yards in 98 attempts, for an average of fewer than 3 yards per carry, and he scored four touchdowns. As a triple-threat, Taliaferro passed for 550 yards in the 1948 season. He was the team MVP and was named All-Big Ten. He was also named first-team All-American in 1948, making him the only Indiana University football player to be named to All-American teams in three different seasons.

IU football may not have lived up to everyone's expectations in 1948, but sports history was still being made at Indiana University. Bill Garrett, a forward for Indiana University, became the first African American to play Big Ten basketball. Unlike Big Ten football, which had some black players, Big Ten basketball did not have a single black player. According to *Getting Open* by Tom Graham and Rachel Graham Cody, there had been some speculation that Indiana's Mr. Basketball of 1946, Johnny Wilson, a black player for state champion Anderson High School, would play for IU and become

George Taliaferro doing another pose, this one in October 1948, his last year with the Hoosiers. A triple threat, Taliaferro could run, pass, and kick, and he played both offense and defense. *Photo courtesy IU Archives.*

The starters for the 1948 Hoosiers. George Taliaferro is the first player from the right in the second row. This was his first year under new coach Clyde Smith. *Photo courtesy IU Archives.*

the first black basketball player in the Big Ten. President Wells was open to the idea, but the gentlemen's agreement that existed among Big Ten coaches kept this from happening. Similar circumstances happened the following year with Bill Garrett. Garrett led Shelbyville to a state championship and was named Indiana's Mr. Basketball of 1947. Rumors circulated that he would break the color barrier in Big Ten basketball, but for a while it looked like history would repeat itself. No Big Ten basketball coaches were present at Shelbyville's April 2 celebration. In typical fashion, however, Indiana University Football Coach Bo McMillin attended and was even the keynote speaker, willing as always to take a stand for what was right. With pressure from several sources, including IU president Wells, Coach Branch McCracken challenged the status quo in Big Ten basketball and recruited Bill Garrett, breaking the gentlemen's agreement that had kept Wilson from playing in the Big Ten.

Also significant that year were the strides Taliaferro was making in his personal life. In December, while she was visiting an aunt in Cleveland, Taliaferro was able to visit Viola Jones. He proposed to her in her aunt's living room, with both the engagement and wedding ring, and this time, to his utter delight, she accepted. Jones, however, was not as convinced as Taliaferro about his decision to leave school. Although she felt that it was her fiancé's decision to make, she could not understand it. She could not imagine why anyone who had the opportunity to get an education would decline it. Her parents, like Taliaferro's, valued education. They regularly attended Parent/Teacher Association (PTA) meetings and her father had even been its president at one time. She did not like the idea of him quitting school, because she was not as convinced as he was that he would actually go back.

Taliaferro finished out the 1948–1949 school year. He had attended Indiana University for three years, and had made a lasting impression. He had not only endured the racism and segregation that existed in Bloomington, Indiana, but he had fought against it and helped integrate restaurants and movie theaters. Taliaferro had also helped his team achieve an undefeated season and Big Ten championship in 1945. Few would forget The Run in 1947. He was a letter winner all three seasons, and had been selected in 1949 for the College All-Star game in Chicago against the Philadelphia Eagles. The College All-Star game was a contest between the best graduated college seniors and the defending NFL champions. The All-Star game was sponsored by *Chicago Tribune* sports editor Arch Ward as a charity fundraiser. At the 1949 game 93,780 spectators watched the Eagles stuff the All-Stars 38 to 0. Playing for the Eagles was Taliaferro's former Indiana teammate Pete Pihos. Two years earlier, friend Buddy Young from Illinois had been the game MVP. While fan interest obviously wasn't a problem, the players' fear of injury and the almost guaranteed win by the NFL team eventually brought the game to a halt. When the tradition ended after the game in 1976, the NFL had the series with a 31-9-2 record.

With the College All-Star game officially ending his college football career, it was time for Taliaferro to put his football skills to the true test: the pro arena. He was finally ready to pursue his professional career to help his mother, despite the misgivings of the woman he loved.

Integrating Professional Football

To appease college coaches who were tired of losing players to the professional leagues, Joe Carr, NFL president from 1921 to 1939, passed a rule forbidding any professional team from signing a player before his class graduated. This meant that Taliaferro had to wait until the class he started with in college graduated before he would be eligible to play professional football. Because of his stint in the army, he was not graduating in 1949. But his class was, making him eligible to play professional football.

Although it was not time for him to graduate, it *was* time for him to make history. The morning of the NFL draft, Taliaferro, who had since moved back to Gary, had been working out in Chicago with friends Buddy Young, Earl Banks, and Sherman Howard. Their shared love of football and similar experiences in the Big Ten had led to a close friendship among the four men. One of those Big Ten games had pitted Indiana against Iowa, for whom Banks played. Taliaferro remembered that, when the opportunity presented itself, he had walked across the field to greet his friend. The response surprised him.

"Shut up and play," Banks had growled.

The game was resuming, so Taliaferro didn't have a chance to respond. As soon as it ended, however, he headed back over to Banks.

"Why are you in such a bad mood?" he asked, half laughing, trying to get a smile out of his friend.

"Why won't they let me sleep in the hotel?" Banks had replied. His team, which had come to Bloomington the day before, had stayed in a whites-only hotel. Banks had been forced to spend the night in Indianapolis and make the hour and a half drive early that morning.

Taliaferro had understood.

It was these past experiences that had created such a strong bond between the men. After college, they had all come to live in the Chicago area and often worked out together. To Taliaferro, workouts were also a learning opportunity because Banks, Howard, and Young were already playing pro ball. Although they sometimes worked out in Gary, they happened to be in Chicago one day, and their workout had lasted from 9:00 that morning until about 11:00. Afterwards, they decided to go out for a quick lunch. Howard, Young, and Taliaferro were going to shower and change at the gym, and Banks would run home to change and meet them at the restaurant.

Banks walked up to the table where the other three were already sitting. "Guess who was drafted by the Bears?" he asked, a smirk playing at the corners of his mouth. The others didn't notice, but he was trying to keep from smiling, trying to keep the secret from leaping out before he could tease them with it. They all began to guess, throwing out the names of players they thought were possible candidates. They were all white players, of course. Banks kept shaking his head, smiling. Finally, unable to contain it any longer, he unfolded a copy of *The Chicago Defender* he had hidden behind his back. In three-inch block letters were the history-making words: George Taliaferro Is "Drafted" by Chicago Bears.

Taliaferro was speechless. His mouth was open but it was not moving, and no sound was escaping his lips. *This has to be a joke,* he thought, alternately looking from the headline to his friends. The Chicago Bears, just two years after Jackie Robinson broke the color barrier in baseball, broke an unwritten NFL rule and picked Taliaferro in the thirteenth round of the 1949 draft, making him the first black man to be drafted by a National Football League team. Until 1949, the black players in the NFL were present only through tryouts.

Before the draft, Bo McMillin, who was coaching the Detroit Lions, had also been hoping to sign Taliaferro. According to Harry Warren, "Halas and Coach A.N. McMillin engaged in a lively battle for George Taliaferro, Negro halfback from Indiana University. . . . McMillin was anxious to get the Gary speedster because he had coached him at Indiana. . . ." Unable to acquire the former IU star, McMillin was at least able to get another 1945 Indiana player, Mel Groomes.

Ironically, George "Papa Bear" Halas, who played, coached, and owned the Bears since the club's inception, had possibly played an influential role in segregating the NFL even earlier, in the 1930s. African American coach Fritz Pollard blamed Halas for keeping him out of the league in the '30s and '40s. An article in *The Chicago Defender* hinted that drafting Taliaferro was a different experience for the Bears: "Not since the days of Fred Duke Slater, former All-American tackle at the University of Iowa, . . . and Joe Lillard, have any Negroes played on any Chicago teams in the National Pro League." It continued, "The Negro stars, for some reason or other, never 'made' the Bears' teams."

Like Taliaferro, Halas had also been a Big Ten football player, leading the University of Illinois to a Big Ten title in 1918. Also like Taliaferro, he spent time during his college career in the service, serving in the Navy during World War I. Aside from playing football for Illinois coach Bob Zuppke, Halas also played baseball and basketball for the Illini, going on to play semi-pro baseball. It was his association with a starch manufacturer, A. E. Staley, however, that would lead to his vital role in the NFL. As a player and coach of the company's football team, Halas elected to use the blue and orange colors of his college alma mater for the team uniforms. In 1920, he represented the company at a meeting in Canton, Ohio, which led to the formation of the National Football League. Staley's starch company was awarded a franchise, and they chose the name "Decatur Staleys."

The Staleys did well that first season, going 10-2-1, but it was a difficult season financially. The Staleys moved to Chicago and won the NFL championship in 1921, then changed the name to the Bears in honor of the Chicago Cubs who had allowed them to play their games at Wrigley Field. Halas became a permanent and influential fixture in the NFL. His career with the Bears lasted decades.

For Taliaferro, who grew up just outside of Chicago, to play for the Bears would fulfill a childhood dream. When the Bears drafted him, however, Taliaferro had already verbally agreed to play for the Los Angeles Dons in the All-America Football Conference. Now he had a decision to make. He could fulfill his dream of playing for the Bears or honor his contract. He decided to talk to his mother about the difficult decision. She had been his best friend growing up and the one person he could talk to about anything. Neither her lack of formal education nor her mildness had kept her from being the family doctor, lawyer, cook, and, while Taliaferro was in high school, the occasional moderator between him and his father. Still relying on her for advice, he called her and explained the situation. He had signed with the Dons, he said, but that was before the Bears came calling. Gary, while in Indiana, was just on the outskirts of Chicago, so there was loyalty to Chicago teams by Gary fans. He remembered telling his sandlot football teammates that someday he would play for the Bears. They all thought he was crazy. So when the impossible happened and the Bears drafted him, Taliaferro was tempted to sign. Still, his mother reminded him, being honest and keeping one's word was of the utmost importance.

"A man's word is his bond," she said, repeating the words his father had said to him so many times during his youth. Convinced, Taliaferro gave up his childhood dream on principle (although it didn't hurt that the Dons' salary offer was a little higher) and he signed the contract with the Los Angeles Dons. "The announcement did not disclose the price, but the consensus was that the Negro star did all right because there has been a financial tug-of-war between the Dons and the Chicago Bears for his services," a *Chicago Daily Tribune* article stated. Taliaferro's situation was typical of the NFL and AAFC war. Harry Sheer, of *The Chicago Daily News,* wrote: "Reports trickling in from the football marts indicate that the All-America has taken the offensive in grabbing off all the talent it can lay its hands on . . . big names or not." He continued to list the players, including Taliaferro, who were snatched up by the AAFC. Seymour Shub, of the *Chicago Sun Times,* however, reported that Halas wasn't too upset with Taliaferro's decision. He'd planned to wait to sign Taliaferro until 1950 anyway, because he knew Taliaferro still had one year left of college eligibility. While Taliaferro retained the honor of being the first African American drafted by an NFL team, when he declined the Bears' offer, Wally Triplett, a halfback from Penn State who was picked in the nineteenth round of the 1949 draft, became the first African American draftee to actually play in the NFL. Triplett was drafted by none other than Coach Bo McMillin.

Whether Taliaferro played for the Bears or the Dons was irrelevant to Indiana University fans, who either way mourned the fact that Taliaferro wouldn't be playing another year for the Hoosiers. An article in the *Chicago Defender* on January 8, 1949, probably sums it up best: "Gloom weighs like a ton on Bloomington. Big George is gone. Not that the University of Indiana [Indiana University] expected to field a championship football team next fall, they just hoped to hold their own. But Big George Taliaferro of Gary was their team." Taliaferro had scored two-thirds of Indiana's total points and had played 40 minutes in each game of the 1948 season. Indiana University was losing its key player on both offense and defense.

To Taliaferro the $7,000 contract and $4,000 signing bonus he was getting from the Dons was "all the money in the world." As a very young boy, he had often told his mother she would never have to worry about anything. He had quit school to fulfill that promise, and now it was happening. He was going to take care of the woman who had always taken care of him, and he began by buying her a house. George Taliaferro was a professional football player.

He did not forget the promise he made to his mother after the Purdue game, though, and the contract stated that he would return to Indiana University to finish his degree.

Being the first black man drafted by an NFL team was not the only trailblazing that Taliaferro was doing in 1949. As usual, he was trying to erase the color lines that criss-crossed nearly every aspect of his life. When Taliaferro started for the Dons, a team that played a wing-T formation, he continued to play in the quarterback/tailback position, making him the first black quarterback to play professional football. Professional football, however, was notoriously slow to change, and while the two large strides made by Taliaferro did not quickly integrate the league, it did help to open the door for other black players.

Before starting his professional football career, Taliaferro had one more collegiate task, to play in the College All-Star game in Chicago in August. The College All-Stars played against the Philadelphia Eagles. Proud of his accomplishment, he wanted Viola Jones to come to the game to watch him play. She turned down his offer. She was working in Washington, D.C., and could not make it to the game, she said. This started an argument, with Taliaferro not understanding why she wouldn't make the trip and Jones not understanding why he was making it such a big deal. By the time they hung up, words had been exchanged, neither one having changed their position on the matter. Taliaferro then wrote a letter to her indicating his displeasure with the situation. This served only to make matters worse. In response, Jones simply returned his engagement ring. Although her response to his second marriage proposal was positive, the results were the same. George Taliaferro was not going to be married to Viola Jones.

Saddened, Taliaferro was at least able to keep himself distracted by working during the summer. Because professional football players in the 1940s did not sign million-dollar contracts or lucrative endorsement deals, most of the players had other jobs during the off season. Taliaferro and another pro football player from Gary, John Brown, worked in construction for a man named Jeter Means. Means expected more work and better results from his two football players than from the rest of his employees. They were, after all, supposed to be stronger and faster than the other men, he had decided. Taliaferro and Brown worked even harder than usual one day filling up the boards for the bricklayers. They would bring the bricks and put them on the hod, a V-shaped apparatus for carrying bricks. When it was full, they would walk up the ladder, take the bricks from the hod and put them on a board near the brick layer, who would then never have to stop laying to find a brick. It was hot, exhausting work, and it must have shown on their faces. Means called out to them, "Taliaferro and Big John, give out, don't give up, because all sickness ain't death." Taliaferro would adopt this phrase as a personal mantra.

The time went by quickly despite the grunt work, and it was soon time to join the Los Angeles Dons for his rookie year. One of his first games was against New York. Although the Dons had lost 17 to 16, Taliaferro had given it his all. The next day an article in *The Chicago Tribune* said, "Los Angeles almost tied the score in the final thirty seconds when George Taliaferro, ex-Indiana star, returned a punt 52 yards for a touchdown." Unfortunately, the extra point that would have tied the game was blocked. Earlier in the game, Taliaferro also had a 44-yard run and some successful passing plays. It looked like the Dons would be getting their money's worth. After New York, the Dons went to Hershey, Pennsylvania, to prepare for their next game against the Cleveland Browns. Taliaferro and Jones, in the meantime, had patched things up. While he was in Hershey, they tried to set a date for him to come to Washington, D.C., so they could get married. But it was not to be. There was not enough time, it was too far away, and there was a clause in his contract that forbade marriage during the rookie season. Taliaferro was starting to wonder if he would ever marry Viola.

He continued playing football, something that remained a constant in his life even when other aspects of it weren't going well. About midway through the season, Taliaferro had an especially impressive game against the Baltimore Colts. Before the game his teammates had warned him about the Baltimore fans. "If you have to run out of bounds, get back in fast," they said. Baltimore did not have a major league baseball team, nor did it have any other professional team to follow. All of their energy was poured into supporting their Colts. With the stadium under construction, these zealous fans could crowd very close to the field. Taliaferro could feel the crowd's energy as soon as he stepped onto the field, but by the end of the game they had also felt his.

Journalist Sam Banks wrote about his performance for the magazine *Our Sports*. Taliaferro appeared on the cover in a classic football pose, left arm wrapped around the football tucked into his body, right arm out ready to stiff arm anyone in his way. He appeared to be bursting through the cover of the magazine. Above his picture were the words: Jackie Robinson, Editor—clearly alluding to the historic connection between the two men. In the article, Banks wrote about Taliaferro: "The powerfully-built charger had what may have been his finest day in professional football. He passed, ran and punted the Dons to a lop-sided win over the Colts, and the thousands

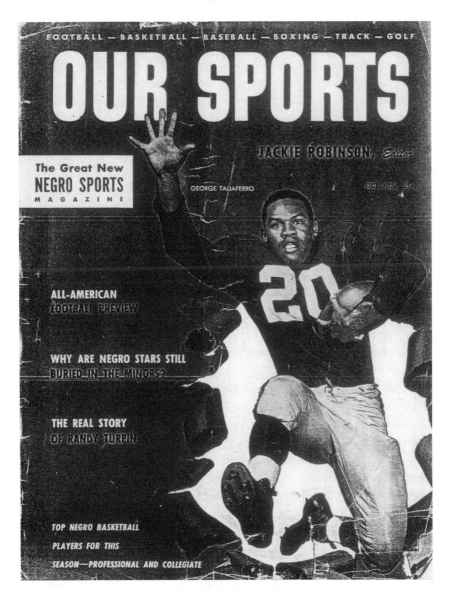

Taliaferro bursts out of the cover of the October/November 1953 issue of *Our Sports*, a magazine for black college and professional athletes that was edited by none other than Jackie Robinson. *Photo courtesy George Taliaferro.*

of fans who witnessed his performance went away 'oohing and ahing' and bemoaning the fact that Taliaferro was not a member of the under-manned Colts." Banks added: "His brilliant offensive play that day was nothing short of magnificent. And his defensive work only went to point up his all-around brilliance. For example, on two occasions he got off spiraling punts that soared some sixty yards, and then raced down the field to make the tackles himself."

In October, Taliaferro met another former Indiana player, Bob Hoernschemeyer, when the Dons played the Chicago Hornets. The game, not to be taken lightly, would decide which team would win a playoff berth in the All-America Conference. As he had so often done in the course of his football career, Taliaferro delivered. Robert Cromie of the *Chicago Daily Tribune* wrote the next day: "George Taliaferro, former Indiana All-American, last night made a strong bid for rookie-of-the-year honors as he passed the Los Angeles Dons to a 24 to 14 victory over the Chicago Hornets. . . ." Taliaferro scored two touchdowns, had 15 carries for 48 yards, and passed 12 of 24 for 215 yards.

It is no wonder then that he finished his rookie year with the Dons with post-season honors. He was, as Cromie predicted, selected Rookie of the Year in the AAFC. He had had a promising season in which, according to Banks, his total offense covered 1,249 yards, making him the leading rookie in the AAFC, and winning him the honor of outstanding rookie back. He was also the number two rusher with 472 yards, number two scorer with 42 points, and number two kickoff return man with 313 yards. He had even run one punt back for a touchdown. He was enjoying his success in professional football, but he was also enjoying living in Los Angeles. The fact that the Dons had recruited other African American players helped put him at ease in his new environment.

Almost as quickly as it had begun, however, Taliaferro's career with the Dons was over. According to Peterson, by 1948, all of the AAFC teams, except for the Browns, were losing money. The ongoing player war with the NFL did not help matters. Edward Prell, a Chicago journalist, wrote in April of 1948: "One of the biggest headaches these days to professional football and baseball operators is the ever-recurring bonuses star athletes ask [for] before they sign on the dotted line." Taliaferro's $4,000 bonus was a large sum of money in 1949. Prell said the bonuses were a product of the NFL and AAFC war for players. By the end of that 1949 season the Dons had been given back to the AAFC by its owners because the team was financially devastated. The only two stable teams in the struggling league were the Browns and the

49ers, but even their attendance was down, indicating trouble to come. Still, this did not keep the two leagues from continuing their fight for players and for position. The AAFC commissioner went so far as to challenge the NFL to a playoff game. He wanted the champion of each league to play for the world championship title. The NFL continued its policy of ignoring the AAFC—and the challenge. This, however, did not make it go away. As well as vying for players with the rival league, the NFL was also having attendance problems. It became clear, Peterson wrote, that the two leagues would have to work out something and merge if professional football was to survive.

On December 20, 1948, an article in the *Gary Post-Tribune* alluded to a merger. "Pro Grid Peace Meeting Today" was the title of the article, but all anyone seemed to know about the meeting was that there was one. Once again, it looked like the two leagues were having a hard time communicating. Both leagues had ended their seasons the previous day. The Philadelphia Eagles were the NFL champions after beating the Chicago Cardinals. In the AAFC, the Cleveland Browns had beaten the Buffalo Bills for the title. The article discussed the rumored world championship game between the two and even mentioned that it was scheduled for December 26 in New York. Newspapers the next day offered only a little more information. The meeting was, according to the article, the first between representatives from both leagues. It was actually the first time the NFL had even acknowledged the existence of its rival.

Once again, however, the two leagues were unable to resolve their differences. Instead of a merger, the AAFC commissioner indicated that the two leagues were still on their own and that the AAFC would now be reduced from eight teams to seven. Instead of playing in two divisions, the teams in the league would play a round-robin schedule. In January 1949, Edward Prell wrote, "The All-America's surprise announcement of a seven team setup after four days of mysterious deliberations stamped out the last flicker of hope that peace would be attained with the National League." Because both leagues were losing money to the player and attendance war, it was assumed that at least a common player draft would happen in the hopes of saving both leagues. This did not happen either. According to Prell, Washington Redskins president George Marshall said, "I prefer to let the All-America go another year. They will only get more tired." Marshall was right; nearly a year later the two leagues were finally forced by their financial burdens to come to an agreement.

Before the 1950 season began, the All-America Football Conference ended up merging with the National Football League. An article in the December 10, 1949, *Chicago Daily Tribune* read: "Professional football's four year war was settled across a conference table today. The All-America Conference merged with the National Football League." The war, the article explained, had cost owners from both sides more than two million dollars because of the salary enticements and battle for attendance in cities where the two leagues were in direct competition. Horace Stoneham, owner of the New York Giants baseball team, was credited with the merger. He owned the Polo Grounds where the two New York NFL teams played, and he was tired of losing money because of the war between the rival conferences. He asked Bert Bell, NFL commissioner, and J. Arthur Friedlund, AAFC's representative, to meet. Several conferences later, the two leagues were merged. As per the terms of the agreement, the NFL, which was divided into the American Conference and the National Conference, agreed to take the AAFC's Cleveland Browns, San Francisco 49ers, and Baltimore Colts. The rest of the AAFC teams were put into a pool for an NFL draft. The Dons went under financially, so Taliaferro was one of the many players put into the draft. The New York Yankees of the AAFC were among the teams going out of business. Its players were to be distributed between the New York Bulldogs and the Giants—the Bulldogs choosing to rename themselves the Yankees. Taliaferro was the second player drafted to join the New York Yanks of the National Conference in the National Football League in 1950.

During the off-season he stayed in Bloomington and continued to work. He and IU friends Jerry Stuteville and Casimer "Slug" Witucki decided to go to the Indy 500 together on May 30. Stuteville's roommate was also planning to go. Witucki was one of Taliaferro's football teammates and Stuteville, who was going to do the driving, played basketball for Indiana with Bill Garrett. Leaving around 4:00 AM, they decided, would enable them to beat much of the heavy race traffic. When Taliaferro, awakened by loud banging, answered his door around 3:00 that morning, he noticed immediately that Stuteville, who had just come from a fraternity party, had been drinking. Taliaferro's attempts to get Stuteville to hand over the keys failed. He didn't have a phone to call Witucki, but he thought that if he could get Stuteville to pick him up first and then come back, the two of them could hold their friend down and wrestle the keys from him. When Witucki answered his door a few minutes later, he also noticed that Stuteville had been drinking. Like Taliaferro, he refused to get in the car, opting not to go to the race. Since Witucki wasn't with him, Taliaferro's plan to hold him down wouldn't work. Instead, Taliaferro tried again to reason with him, but Stuteville refused to let anyone else drive. Attempts to keep Stuteville from driving to Indy were

New York Yanks practice. Circa 1950. While with the Yanks, George Taliaferro (#20) has the opportunity to play for the first time with friend Buddy Young (#80). Young, despite being only 5'4", was once the fastest man in the world. Young and Taliaferro shared similar experiences as African American football players on their respective Big Ten teams. *Photo by Bob Olen.*

unsuccessful, so Taliaferro also chose not to go to the race. Stuteville and his roommate left Bloomington without the two football players. Just south of Indianapolis, Stuteville lost control of the car and sideswiped a bridge. Twenty-two and only one month from becoming a college graduate, Jerry Stuteville died instantly. His roommate wasn't injured. Haunted by the fact that he had not been able to keep Stuteville from driving that day, Taliaferro threw himself again into football, the physical effort and familiarity of which was a source of comfort.

Playing for the Yanks in 1950 gave Taliaferro the opportunity to play for the first time with Claude "Buddy" Young, who had been signed by the New York Yanks in 1947. Aside from their shared Big Ten experiences, Young and Taliaferro had also played against each other in high school, when Young had played for one of the few schools against whom the Gary Roosevelt Panthers were permitted to compete—Wendell Phillips High School in Chicago.

Young was "a little guy," Taliaferro recalled. "He was about 5'4" and weighed about 175 pounds. But he could flat out run. At one time Buddy Young was the fastest man in the world," Taliaferro said. Young had, in fact, held the world record for the 45-yard dash and had twice equaled the record for the 60-yard dash while on the track team at the University of Illinois. A Colts football program would later describe Young: "Rated as the toughest man to defense in the league, speedy Buddy is the breakaway runner which gives an attack balance and deception. . . . At just 5 ft. 4 in. he is the shortest player currently active and, because of his stature, is jokingly described as the only man in the world who can block you at the knees without bending down."

Young's experiences paralleled Taliaferro's in many ways. Like Taliaferro, Buddy Young had been a star athlete for an all-black high school in the Midwest. He, too, had gone on to be an All-American for a Big Ten school, playing football and running track for Illinois. Young and his Illinois teammates won the 1946 Big Ten championship and the 1947 Rose Bowl, their only Big Ten loss coming at the hands of Indiana. The 1945 Hoosiers were the last Big Ten champions before the league reached an agreement that would send its championship team to the Rose Bowl. Illinois had had problems with returning servicemen and suffered losses to Indiana and Michigan in 1945, prompting discussions of firing their coach. But by 1946 things were looking up again for the Fighting Illini. Military service during World War II affected both Indiana and Illinois, and both Young and Taliaferro had stints in the service in the middle of their college careers. Playing professional football and raising families were other similarities the two men would eventually share. The racism and segregation that defined their lives was an experience both men managed to overcome with a dignity that made them role models for others. It was no surprise then, that they were close friends.

In college, Young too had been forced to live in a private residence because of the University of Illinois's segregated housing policy. He lived at the home of Mrs. Ida Wells and her husband, a railroad worker who inspired the young men who lived in his home to be successful and hard working. The residents of the Wells' home were all black, male students, but Young was the only athlete. Later, in a 1967 interview, Young would describe athletics as "great equalizers." Sports, he believed, would help realize the constitutional ideal of equality. Like Taliaferro, experiences with white teammates were not always positive. During the first team shower at Illinois, one white teammate waited five minutes, watching Young and a black teammate, Paul Patterson, before finally deciding he could get in the shower. Unlike Taliaferro, Young quit college after his sophomore year to go pro, and he never went back.

GEORGE TALIAFERRO

Halfback—New York Yanks
Age: 23; Residence, Gary, Ind.
Height: 5-11   Weight: 195

This will be George's first year with Yanks. As rookie tailback with Los Angeles Dons last year, led all AAFC frosh in total offense with 1,294 yards. No. 2 rusher with 472 yards, scorer with 42, and kickoff return man with 313. No. 6 major college punter, U. of Indiana, 1948. All-American, 1948. All-Big Ten for 4 years.

No. 14 in a SERIES OF FOOTBALL PICTURE CARDS
© 1950 Bowman Gum, Inc., Phila., Pa., U. S. A.

This 1950 Bowman football card is of George Taliaferro during his first season with the New York Yanks.

While with the Yanks in that 1950 football season, Taliaferro gained 411 yards rushing and scored four touchdowns, tying friend Sherman Howard's record. He also had five touchdowns as a receiver, completed three of seven passes for 83 yards, and threw one touchdown pass. As usual, he played both offensive and defensive positions. In December, he broke a record with eight kickoff returns in the game against the New York Giants. According to the Banks article, it was also during that season that Taliaferro began to earn the reputation of being a "hot-and-cold" player. His coach, Jimmy Phelan, who had been the head coach at Purdue for eight seasons, could tell what kind of a game he was going to have simply by his behavior at practice. If his manner was tense and nervous, Taliaferro would have a good game. A relaxed Taliaferro, however, often meant a lackluster performance was to come. "Nevertheless, the slashing speedster managed to have enough good days to keep his rating as one of the finest runners in the game and, although his passing and punting fell off considerably, he could still pick 'em up and lay 'em down with the best," Banks wrote in *Our Sports* magazine. At the end of the season, the Yanks were seven and five, finishing in third place in the National Division.

Phelan was not always happy with Taliaferro, though. During one practice Taliaferro threw a pass with his left hand instead of his right hand. He was playing halfback in the "T" formation. The quarterback received the ball and threw it to Taliaferro, who was then supposed to throw it to the receiver.

He did, but being ambidextrous, he instinctively threw the ball with his left hand. "I don't want any Globetrotters on my football team," Phelan yelled in disapproval.

About halfway through the season, Milton Purvis made a visit to New York to see Taliaferro. The two men attended football practice, went out to lunch, and took in a movie. Much had happened since Taliaferro had left the army, so the two had a lot of catching up to do as well. One topic, which seemed to be just below the surface of their conversation, did not come up. After dinner, Purvis finally asked what he had been wondering about all day. "When are you going to marry my play sister?" he asked. Taliaferro wished he knew. He had been wondering that also, frustrated by all of the times he had almost married her, only to meet disappointment. Purvis's question prompted him to take action. He was ready to make it permanent, to set the date, but he was nervous. Later that night, Taliaferro had mustered up enough courage to call her, to finally get a definite answer. Sometime after 11:00 that night he picked up the phone and dialed the number. The phone rang at the other end. Taliaferro's heart beat faster. Jones's roommate, Estelle, answered, but before she would put Jones on the phone, she gave Taliaferro grief about waking her up and making phone calls in the middle of the night. After hearing a sufficient apology from him, she reluctantly agreed to wake Jones.

The line went quiet long enough for him to wonder if she hadn't just put the phone down, with no intention of getting Jones at all. Just when he was about to give up, he heard a familiar voice.

"Hello?" She didn't say it; she asked it like a question. He could hear the sleep in her voice, a deeper, rougher version of the familiar one.

Taliaferro identified himself, but he had to ask quickly before he lost his nerve. "Will you marry me?" he asked her for the third time since he had known her.

There was another uncomfortable pause, and then "Yes." She would work it out and call him later with all of the details, she said.

After the phone call, Taliaferro went to bed contented that Jones would soon, finally, be his wife. She fell back asleep immediately, and when she woke up the next morning, she was not even sure if the conversation had taken place. She thought she had talked to Taliaferro, but couldn't be certain. Two thoughts were running through her mind: *I must be dreaming* and *I must be out of my mind.* She picked up the phone and called Taliaferro to ask whether they had talked the previous night.

The ringing telephone woke Taliaferro around 7:00 the next morning.

He shook the sleep off quickly when he realized that it was Jones, and she sounded a little worried. She wanted to know if he had actually called her the night before. She thought perhaps she had just been dreaming and wanted to make sure that was not the case. In case she had been dreaming, she didn't ask what she really wanted to know: had he asked her to marry him? Picking up on this, Taliaferro's worry quickly turned to amusement as he played along.

"What did we discuss?" she asked, once he had confirmed that the call had not been a figment of her imagination.

"I asked you to marry me," he reminded her, matter-of-factly.

"What was my reply?" she asked.

He repeated the conversation for her, reminding her that she was going to work out the details and call him.

"I just wanted to be sure," she said and hung up the phone. Taliaferro smiled.

She did work out the details, and on November 24, 1950 (the fifth anniversary of the game in which Indiana beat Purdue for the unchallenged Big Ten championship), at 3:45 in the afternoon (the same time the game started), George Taliaferro married Viola Jones at her sister's home, with Milton Purvis standing as Taliaferro's best man. Despite several failed attempts, Viola Jones finally became Mrs. Viola Taliaferro. "It took a while for her to realize that life really couldn't go on for me without her," Taliaferro said of the delay. She alluded to this as well. "I don't know. He just came after me. That's all," she said of her decision to marry him. After the nuptials, the newlyweds lived together in Gary for the rest of the football season.

Incidents of racism were fairly isolated while Taliaferro played for the Yanks in 1950. Teammate Sherman Howard said in a 2003 interview that racism was not a problem for him, George Taliaferro, or the other black players on that team. Jim Crow laws continued to beleaguer the black athletes, who still had to stay in separate facilities, often with private families, when the team played games in places like Louisiana and Texas. That, however, was neither new nor unexpected. Most of their Yanks teammates, Howard said, many of whom were from the south, accepted them. Because of their past football experiences, many of their teammates had already heard about Howard and Taliaferro. The players who did not already know them quickly found that these black men, despite having come from neighborhoods generally poorer than their own, were gentlemen with strong values. Howard found that in their relationships with others, he and Taliaferro were often judged by the content of their character, rather than by their skin color.

George and Viola Taliaferro cut their wedding cake on November 24, 1950, the fifth anniversary of the win against Purdue that earned the Hoosiers a Big Ten championship and undefeated season. The Taliaferros were married at 3:45 in the afternoon, the same time the game had started. *Photo courtesy George Taliaferro.*

However isolated, there were still some incidents. One such experience Taliaferro remembered occurred while he played for the Yanks. In a game against San Francisco, Taliaferro had a confrontation with a 49er from Louisiana State University who, Taliaferro said, had not had much experience playing against black football players. Getting that kind of experience, apparently, was making him altogether unhappy. This particular player caught a kick, and as Taliaferro approached to tackle him, the 49er jumped up and tried to kick him in the face. Blocking the player's foot with his forearm, Taliaferro then proceeded to flip him onto his back and punch him in the jaw. The stunned 49er lay on the field as Taliaferro walked away, already readying himself for the next play. "Then it was over," Taliaferro said of the incident.

Taliaferro continued to rack up successful statistics. Howard said he was involved in almost every play of every game. "I would block for him and he would block for me. It wasn't one for one, it was one for all," he said. Howard noticed that Taliaferro had a lot of pride and a strong belief in excellence. "Whatever he does he wants to be the best, and he instills that in others, too," he explained. If they needed a pass or a play, Taliaferro would tell him, "I'm going to do my part, you just do yours." One of the reasons for their strong bond may have been the attitude both men had toward racism. Howard almost echoed Taliaferro when he said of racist people, "They the person got a problem—when I start acting like him then I got a problem—just be yourself."

Before Taliaferro's eyes, football was continuing to evolve, and in 1950, while he and Howard played for the Yanks, professional football became a televised sport. Years later, at breakfast one morning, Viola Taliaferro told their daughters how their daddy had been a football player before there was television. "Mommy, there wasn't anything before television," Renée, their second-oldest daughter replied. Other changes in pro football were also occurring in the 1950s. The experimental rule permitting unlimited substitutions, for example, was made permanent, which also led to the universal practice of having separate teams for offense and defense and the development of specialists like place kickers and punters. Unlike most professional football players, however, Taliaferro continued to play on both sides of the football.

When the 1950 season was over, the Yanks had a record of 7 and 5, and the Taliaferros moved to Bloomington, Indiana. In May of 1951, Taliaferro finally fulfilled the promise he had made to his father and mother and earned his bachelor's degree. Satisfied by this accomplishment, Taliaferro was ready to focus completely on football during the 1951 season. He was with the Yanks again and making history again. Bob Gill, in an article for the newsletter of the Professional Football Researchers Association, wrote that Taliaferro and three other players shared the quarterback position during the 1951 football season after their quarterback, George Ratterman, defected to Canada. Taliaferro, who completed 13 of 33 passes for 251 yards and one touchdown, became the first African American to quarterback in the National Football League.

In the article, Gill called Taliaferro a "forgotten" trailblazer. Willie Thrower, who quarterbacked three games for the Bears in 1953, was sometimes mistakenly given the credit, Gill wrote, for being the first black quarterback in the NFL. On October 18, 1953, George Halas put Thrower in to replace quarterback George Blanda. Thrower completed three of eight passes for 27 yards. His longest gain was 12 yards. He also threw one interception. This

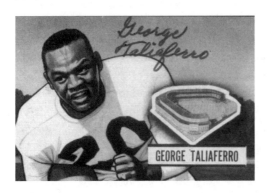

A 1951 Bowman football card of George Taliaferro during his second season with the Yanks.

historic game is, according to some research, the one in which Thrower became the first black quarterback in the NFL. Taliaferro had already been in
the NFL for two years by that time and had thrown 96 passes in the league
before Thrower had even joined the Bears. Still, Taliaferro thinks Thrower
deserves the recognition of being the first African American quarterback
in the NFL. This, Taliaferro says, is because Thrower was actually selected
for the Bears as a quarterback. In an article he wrote for *The Coffin Corner,*
Taliaferro explained: "The Bears listed Willie as quarterback on their roster.
That's important. Because of the variety of plays used in a game and the
changes caused by free substitution, a player might begin a play at almost
any position. But, whatever a team lists as a player's position is what the
team and his coach thought his position was. The Bears thought of Willie as
a quarterback." Taliaferro went on to explain that even though he often took
snaps in what is now known as the shotgun formation, he did not take snaps
under center, which is "the thing that distinguishes a modern T-quarterback
from those who came before." In the single-wing formation, which turned
100 years old in 2006, the ball can be snapped to the tailback, the fullback,
and sometimes a wingback. Taliaferro was a halfback who sometimes played
the quarterback position. "The distinction of being the first black quarterback really does belong to Thrower," he said.

Thrower was more aptly named for the position if nothing else. Maybe two firsts actually occurred that give them both the recognition they deserve. George Taliaferro, it would seem, was the first African American to play quarterback in the NFL, and Thrower was the first African American quarterback in the NFL. Either way, Thrower, who was not accustomed to sitting on the bench, ended up leaving the National Football League to play in the Canadian League for the Toronto Argonauts and the Winnipeg Blue Bombers.

More important to him than his football achievements was the birth of Taliaferro's first daughter. Linda Taliaferro was born in Washington, D.C., on September 28, 1951. Taliaferro was across the country playing a football game in Los Angeles against the Rams. At least something good happened that night because in the game, which did not go well, Taliaferro established a single-game record of 14 punts. That statistic was indicative of the team's season in general; the Yanks came in last place in their division with a record of 1 and 9. The Rams, on the other hand, won the NFL championship.

On the Los Angeles Rams that year was rookie Len Teuuws. Because there were only 15 black players in the NFL and six of them played for the Rams, Teuuws said that they were often called the "Black Rams." Among the six black players were Harry Thompson of UCLA, Bob Boyd of Loyola, and Hall-of-Famer Dick "Night Train" Lane. Lane actually preferred to be called Richard, Teuuws said, "But you know you've become a hero when you have a nickname." Even though the black players had separate sleeping facilities when they played games in the south, they were still part of the "family" to the white teammates. When there were team parties, for example, everyone was invited, including the black players, Teuuws said. On the other hand, there were other great black players who were not on the team because there were already "too many" black players. To stress this point Teuuws said, "If Jesus had come down as a black man, he would not have made the team."

Although the Yanks had not fared as well as the Rams, Taliaferro still managed to stand out. *Los Angeles Times*'s Frank Finch wrote: "[Taliaferro] gave one of the greatest solo performances ever. Handicapped by a lackluster supporting cast, Taliaferro gained 172 yards in 12 tries for a 14.3 average, scored two touchdowns (one coming on a 65-yard run) and passed to Bob Celeri for another. He completed three of five passes, caught one himself, averaged 42.55 yards punting and doubled in brass as a defensive halfback." His statistics for the season were no less impressive. He had passed for 251 yards with two touchdowns, rushed for 330 yards with four touchdowns, and had an average gain of 14 yards per reception. He also led the league in kickoff returns. And that was just on offense. On defense, he added four

STATE FAIR
STADIUM
SEPT. 14
SHREVEPORT

25c

New York
Yanks

VS.

Washington
Redskins

A football program from Taliaferro's 1951 season with the New York Yanks. The Redskins were owned by George Preston Marshall, a man some believed responsible for the segregation of the NFL.

GEORGE TALIAFERRO

89 **BACK**
Dallas Texans

Res.: Gary, Ind.
Age: 25
Height: 5-11
Weight: 195

All-American back from Indiana in 1948. Top rookie in 1949, he is now in third year with Texans (formerly Yanks). Used primarily on offense, George, nevertheless, intercepted 4 passes in 1951, with average return of over 18 yards. Led in kickoff returns, 12th in punting.

RECORD FOR LAST SEASON

CARRYING: Attempts, 62; Yards Gained, 330; Average Gain, 5.3.
PASSING: Attempts, 33; Comp., 13; Yds. G., 251; Td. P., 1; Int., 3; Av. G., 7.61.
RECEIVING: Number, 16; Yards Gained, 230; Average Gain, 14.4.
SCORING: Touchdowns, 5; Total Points, 30.

COLLEGE TO PRO **FOOTBALL** PICTURE CARDS
©1952 Bowman Gum Division, Haelan Laboratories, Inc., Philadelphia 44, Pa. Printed in U.S.A.

The Dallas Texans formed when a group of investors bought the financially downtrodden New York Yanks. Taliaferro was then drafted to play for the Dallas Texans, as shown in this 1952 Bowman football card.

interceptions to the list. At the end of the season, Taliaferro was selected to the Pro Bowl, a game which gave him a chance to meet up again with former Indiana teammate Pete Pihos, who was representing Philadelphia in the Pro Bowl and who went on to become a Professional Football Hall-of-Famer.

Rain fell on Bloomington on March 31, 1952, the anniversary of famed Notre Dame coach Knute Rockne's death. It was that same day Bo McMillin, Taliaferro's Indiana University football coach and mentor, died of a heart attack in his Bloomington home. He was 57 years old. He had retired early from coaching the Philadelphia Eagles because of health reasons when two operations were unsuccessful at curing a severe stomach ailment. A month earlier, he had been hospitalized for a few weeks. He had returned home just ten days prior to his death. The city had adopted McMillin, the man they credited with having the largest impact ever on IU athletics. University leaders and former football players were among those who mourned the Texan. They remembered his ability to lead and inspire with colorful aphorisms rolling off his tongue in a Texan drawl. Former players acted as pallbearers for the man who had been such an influence on them. Taliaferro was unable to make it to the funeral, but he mourned the loss of his mentor. McMillin, who had been there for him through some very difficult times, would never be forgotten. In addition to mourning his mentor, Taliaferro was dealing with the continued pressure of playing for a team that was barely surviving.

The end of the 1951 season for the Yanks had not brought an end to the NFL saga, despite its integration with the AAFC. The New York Yanks of 1950 and 1951 folded, and in 1952 became the Dallas Texans. Taliaferro, then, became a Texan. Like its predecessors, the Texans was a team fraught with problems from the outset. In his article "Belly Up in Dallas," Joe Horrigan described the Texans' failings. Yanks owner Ted Collins was tired of spending money on a losing team, so he sold the franchise back to the NFL. That was when Texan millionaire Giles Miller and a group of investors decided to buy the troubled franchise to bring professional football to Dallas. Early on there were critics of the move. Journalist Stan Grosshandler wrote later that some critics worried that a state so devoted to college football would not be supportive of a pro team. Others were just bothered by the losing track record of the Yanks, which would make attracting fan support difficult. On the other hand, supporters of the move thought Dallas was ready for a professional football team precisely because they were so supportive of high school and college football. At the very least, the general consensus was that Dallas was a better bet than Baltimore for the team. The board of directors of the old Baltimore Colts was also bidding on the team, but when the final decision was made, the New York Yanks had become the Dallas Texans, Texas's first professional football team, and Baltimore was still without one.

The critics of the move to Dallas may have been right. While the Texans played in the Cotton Bowl, an arena that seated 75,000 people, on their best day they drew a crowd of only 17,499 people. On opening day a meager 15,000 fans turned out to watch their newly acquired team, Grosshandler wrote. The team's only shining moment of the entire season was a recovered fumble minutes into the opening game that led to a Texan touchdown. After that, things steadily declined. The Giants ended up winning that game 24 to 6, and each week, as the losses piled up, the crowds grew smaller. Coach Phelan even joked that rather than have the players announced over the public address system before the game, they should just go into the stands and personally introduce themselves to each fan. Sadly, in a state that was known for its obsession with football, it was a struggle to get anyone to watch their games.

Giles Miller and his investors were unable to cover the expenses of running the losing Texans, and even before the season was over, they returned the team to the NFL. Rarely getting a chance to stop and practice, and playing all games at the arenas of their opponents, the Texans became a road team without a home. Despite the obstacles his team continued to face as a whole, Taliaferro was still on top of his game. He and Buddy Young were still teammates, and the duo was still dynamite together in the backfield. This, according to Horrigan, was one of the positive aspects of the team. He wrote: "After all, their roster did include future Hall-of-Famers Gino Marchetti and Art Donovan, and the potentially explosive backfield duo of Buddy Young and George Taliaferro." Even though the season had not been going well, Taliaferro's skill was not questioned. In the Los Angeles Rams vs. Dallas Texans football program, Frank Finch wrote about him: "The fact that every club in the National Football League would bid the limit for the former Indiana All-American is ample evidence of his pigskin prowess." At season's end, Taliaferro was, once again, on the Pro Bowl roster for the National Division, his second time. During the season, he had rushed for 419 yards in 100 attempts and had one touchdown. He had also passed for 298 yards and two touchdowns. His average gain receiving was about 12 yards with 244 yards in 21 attempts and one touchdown. His statistics, once again, were impressive despite having played for a losing team which ended its season with a record of 1 and 11.

Life in Dallas, on top of the losses and volatility of the team, was hard for the Taliaferros. The 1950s was a difficult time period for African Americans, Viola Taliaferro said, no matter where one lived. Anywhere in the south, however, was particularly awful. The segregation was worse in Dallas than it had been in the east. She could not even go shopping, she said, and there was not a day in Dallas that she felt they were treated with the respect and equality they deserved. There was not a single day that they were not treated as being inferior in some way. Even the Cotton Bowl, the arena for the Dallas Texans, was segregated. In other arenas, she and Buddy Young's wife, Geraldine Young, would sit with the other wives, but that was not the case at Dallas's Cotton Bowl. There, they sat in the segregated section. When the Texans' owners noticed where the two women were sitting, they invited them to sit in the section with the other players' wives. To make a point, the two women declined the offer, refusing to leave the "colored" section of the field. "No, it is your practice that black people sit together and that is exactly where I am going to sit," Mrs. Taliaferro told them. It was hard, she explained, to experience that kind of thing on a daily basis and not get to a point where she was just filled with hatred.

Originally, a plan had been designed to permanently segregate seating at the Dallas stadium. It was planned, according to Horrigan, in anticipation of the heavy demand for tickets from Dallas's African American fans. But the segregated seating was not permanent. While the exact reason behind this was not determined, there was some speculation. "Whether resulting from

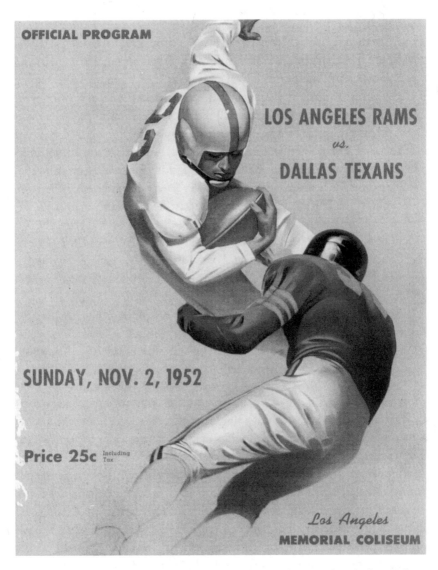

LOS ANGELES RAMS

vs.

DALLAS TEXANS

SUNDAY, NOV. 2, 1952

Price 25c Including Tax

Los Angeles
MEMORIAL COLISEUM

In 1952, the Los Angeles Rams were on their way to the NFL championship. The financially devastated Texans won only one game.

November 23, 1952: Dallas Texans vs. Green Bay Packers. Number 20 on the left is George Taliaferro. Number 44 on the right is Packers rookie Bobby Dillon. *Photo courtesy George Taliaferro.*

pressure from the Texans' management or a lack of ticket requests in general, a minor blow for social justice occurred when segregated seating never materialized," Horrigan wrote. Segregated seating was not the only plan that did not work out for the Texans. Ready to pick up the broken pieces was Baltimore. Although they had been spurned before, the city of Baltimore was still interested in the troubled franchise whose demise they had followed all season. But the NFL still had its reservations and was not convinced the team should move there. If they wanted the financially devastated, homeless football team, they were going to have to prove it, and it wasn't going to be easy. The NFL simply wasn't going to take any more risks.

To acquire the team, then, Baltimore had to meet the NFL's challenge to sell 15,000 season books in a six-week period of time. The books, which cost $19.80, were offered for sale at the worst time of year, around Christmas, the tickets were for games that were nearly a year away, and the team had previously lost all but one game. To top it off, the Colts' previous best advance sale had been 6,700 tickets. Selling 15,000 tickets in six weeks was not going to be easy. But Baltimore was also a city that had kept together the Colts Band, which had continued to meet every Sunday, even during the years when the city did not have a team. The Colt Corrals, the unofficial gathering of Colts fans, also continued, even when the city was Colt-less. Baltimore loved its football team even when it didn't have it; if any city could rise to the challenge, Baltimore would be it.

Any lingering doubts were erased when the city met the challenge in only four weeks and three days. On January 23, 1953, the team that had been the Yanks, and then the Texans, officially became the second edition of the Baltimore Colts.

A Colts team had existed in 1947 in the All-America Football Conference. The first edition of the Colts was formed when the Miami Seahawks folded. Those Colts had dressed in their predecessor's colors, green and silver. In 1950, the team became an NFL member, but it was disbanded after the 1950 season after a losing streak of 18 games over two seasons and a significant loss of money. With the orphaned Dallas Texans seeking a home, Baltimore saw its opportunity to adopt a professional football team again. Since the second edition of the Colts was formed from the Texans, whose colors had been blue, white, and silver, the new Baltimore Colts team opted for those colors. They rarely wore the silver, however, and soon their colors became blue and white. On the sidelines during the game, the players would wear reversible blue hooded capes that were cloth on one side and rain gear on the other. Just visible between the layers was the stitched outline of a star—the Dallas Texans logo. They had simply had a new layer added over it.

While Baltimore was going through the process of acquiring the Colts, the Taliaferros had moved. After their experience living in segregated Dallas, they decided to move back to Los Angeles. While the Los Angeles experience was different than Dallas, it was not necessarily better. And the couple wasn't sure how they would feel about Baltimore. Hesitant to pick up and move everything again only to end up somewhere else they didn't feel like they belonged, they decided to keep a residence in each city until they could be certain that they should move. In July Taliaferro left for Baltimore, and his family stayed in Los Angeles.

The support Baltimore showed when they purchased more than 15,000 season tickets did not wane in the intervening months, and when the Colts started their first season as an NFL team, the Colts Band was waiting for them. The old Colts Band would be playing in a new stadium, one that was being built as a new level above the old one. Ed Steers, who had moved from Philly to Baltimore in 1947, the same year the Colts came to Baltimore for the first time, was a water boy for the second edition of the Colts. He remembers those days well. The upper deck of Baltimore Memorial Stadium was being constructed during the 1953–1954 season because the stadium was also going to be used for baseball.

There were tunnels under the stands for the construction workers to bring in their materials. Steers, who lived just three blocks from the stadium, and his friends had explored every inch of those tunnels. They knew how to sneak into the stadium to watch the Colts on any given day. They also liked to sneak in to watch Notre Dame–Navy games when Navy used the stadium. In 1953, Steers and his friends would sneak in to watch their heroes, players like Buddy Young and George Taliaferro. On one such occasion, when the Colts were playing the Packers, Steers and his cousin discovered, to their utter dismay, that one of the tunnels had been closed off, thus keeping them from sneaking into the game. They weighed their options. They could climb the fence at center field, but it was so high the police would usually catch the kids who were gate crashing before they made it all the way over. Sometimes a group of 40 kids would rush the fence, knowing about 10 of them would make it without getting caught, but that wasn't going to work with just the two of them. They were starting to run out of options, and they could hear the Colts Band playing, signaling that the game would soon begin. Panicked that they were going to miss the game, they ran around to the players' entrance to see if it was open. As they were hanging out by the door waiting to see if they could somehow get in, a taxi pulled up. Out stepped a black man in pajamas, a robe, and leather slippers. They recognized him at once as Buddy Young, the smallest man on the team. They called to him, begging him to let them in the player door. At first Young just looked at the boys in surprise, taking in what they were saying. Then he shook his head, shrugged, and waved them in saying, "Okay, come on."

Young led them to the locker room and asked equipment manager Freddy Shubach to give them something to do. Shubach accommodated him and gave the boys water and towels. Not only had they gotten into the game for free, but they were even able to stand on the sidelines in their new role as water boys. These water boys didn't have paper cups and plastic coolers, though. They scooped water from a galvanized bucket and lifted the metal ladle to the lips of their thirsty heroes. Although it hadn't occurred to him at the time, years later Steers was struck by the fact that Buddy Young had let them into the game that night. "Two white kids, why in the hell should he bother with us? It was such an unusual thing to do, but he said, 'Sure kids, come on,'" Steers recalled. But Buddy Young had a reputation for being charitable, and things like that went on in Baltimore all the time, Steers said. The NFL, even professional sports in general, weren't like they are today, he explained. In the 1950s, the players were accessible to the fans. The Colts were a part of Baltimore, not just something to be worshipped from afar. Steers said he would run into the players at the local pizza parlors and laundromats. Fans would also attend the Colts practices and then sit and talk to the players afterwards. Steers had lived just down the street from Clifton Park, where the Colts held practices during the years 1947 to 1949, and he went to practice every day to watch. He was one of the fans who would stay and talk to players. He also watched when they practiced at Westminster Maryland College.

At this time professional football was struggling, Steers explained. It had nowhere near the following baseball had. Teams used patched-up equipment and played on public fields. "They weren't superstars," Steers explained. They were just guys who had played college football; they all had jobs on the side. They were a part of Baltimore, and the fans knew them. There was a real connection between the fans and the players, who didn't disappoint when they started off the 1953 season well enough to prompt pennant dreams. The Colts already had two wins against the Bears and played a close game with Detroit, the defending champions. Even a disappointing loss to the winless Green Bay Packers, 37-14, wasn't all loss. It actually may have turned out to be a good thing for the Colts.

Watching the game that day was Carroll Rosenbloom, a wealthy textile manufacturer and former collegiate football player. The Penn alum had been persuaded to be the financial backer for the Colts. Rosenbloom had agreed to do so reluctantly and only out of a loyalty he felt to the city. This changed, ironically enough, when he watched the first loss of the season. At the end of the game with no hope of making up for the deficit, Rosenbloom watched George Taliaferro continue to play as if they could still win it. On a Green Bay punt the last play of the game, Taliaferro ran about 40 yards and was tackled just past the Colts bench. Carroll Rosenbloom leaned over and asked him why he hadn't run out of bounds. Taliaferro responded, "That's not how I play football." Rosenbloom was impressed. "Even when they had you cornered . . ." he said, his voice trailing off into thought.

Stuart McIver described the incident for *Sport* magazine: "The game was nearly over and the Colts hopelessly beaten when George Taliaferro, their Negro halfback, ran a punt back for good yardage. He was at the sidelines when the Packers closed in on him. He had only to step out of bounds to avoid the tackle. Instead he piled into the Packers and picked up two extra

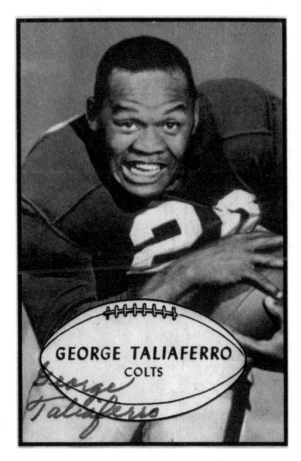

There to pick up the pieces of the Dallas Texans is Baltimore. The city met an NFL challenge and earned the team, making Taliaferro a Baltimore Colt, as seen on this 1953 Bowman football card.

GEORGE TALIAFERRO
COLTS

yards. 'If they want to play that hard,' said Rosenbloom, 'I want to go with them all the way. If they've got that kind of spirit, I can't sit back, can I?'" Rosenbloom came away with a renewed sense of confidence and a total willingness to back his team. The Baltimore fans must have shared Rosenbloom's feelings. When the losing Colts returned to the airport, 4,000 fans were there to greet them. The Colts, for their part, didn't disappoint the following Sunday when they beat the Redskins.

To Taliaferro, the most humorous incident of the season occurred during this Washington Redskins game. It began, he remembered, with a comment by Redskins owner George Preston Marshall, the man who was still refusing to integrate his football team, even though others had already done so. Marshall was standing just behind Taliaferro during the team introductions

This picture appeared in the December 1954 issue of *Sport* magazine. The caption read: "Former Indiana all-purpose back, George Taliaferro has been the team's big gun in recent seasons. He runs, passes, does punting." Taliaferro was still a Baltimore Colt at this time.

and said loudly enough for Taliaferro to hear, "Niggers should never be allowed to do anything but push wheelbarrows." Although the comment itself wasn't funny, Taliaferro had to laugh, "because then I went out and scored three touchdowns!" he said.

Excitement continued to grow as the season progressed. In a late November game against the Rams they played in fog so heavy the players couldn't see from one end of the field to the other. To make matters worse, this was to be Taliaferro's first experience as quarterback for the Colts. Taliaferro supposed his experience at Indiana University, during which he often threw passes as a running back in the old single wing formation, earned him the quarterback position. The Tuesday before, with his other quarterbacks injured, Coach Molesworth, "Moley" as the players called him, had begun preparing Taliaferro for the role. Molesworth focused on a few basic plays during practice to initiate Taliaferro into the quarterback position. They kept practicing these plays until they were confident Taliaferro had them down. Nobody realized at the time that Taliaferro's initiation into the position would include such heavy fog.

The game started with the Colts receiving first. They picked up a first down, and the first series of plays, which had been determined before the game, went smoothly for Taliaferro. But when he got in the huddle to begin the second series, he couldn't remember a single play. He looked at the players in the huddle hoping the plays would come to him, but they didn't. Realizing he was in trouble, he had to call a quick time out. "I can't remember the plays!" he gasped to Coach Molesworth, who burst out in a hearty laugh before grabbing the playbook and refreshing Taliaferro's memory. That was all Taliaferro needed. The second series having been re-introduced to him, he began calling plays like he had been quarterbacking for years. His performance in the heavy fog, which included running, passing, and kicking, could have earned the Colts another win if Taliaferro hadn't thrown a long pass that was picked off to give the Rams a 21 to 13 win. Still, Taliaferro had put on a show and proved he was worthy of the quarterback position. PR director Sammy Banks later wrote about the game, "Who will ever forget the brilliant display put on by George Taliaferro as he took over the quarterbacking chores for the injured Fred Enke? And how about that fog? Remember? You couldn't even see the fans in the upper deck during the second half."

Unfortunately for the Colts and their loyal fans, the pennant dreams had faded by the end of the season. They had made an only slight improvement on the Texans' record with three wins and nine losses, finishing in fifth place in the West Division of the NFL. The record book hadn't recorded the team's other successes, though. The fans had proven they were an NFL city with their record-breaking season ticket purchases. Rosenbloom had been inspired by his team's determination, and it turned out to be the first year the team had finished the season with a profit. The players and coaches were even awarded $500 Christmas bonuses. And Taliaferro had, for the third time in a row, earned a position on the Pro Bowl roster. His triple threat abilities were apparent in his other statistics as well. He rushed for 479 yards that season. His average kickoff return was 19 yards. In the 1953 season, he also established a rushing record of 95 yards for the longest run by a Colt. More important, Taliaferro was happy to add to his family when his second daughter, Renée Angela, was born at around 7:00 PM on December 15, at Cedars of Lebanon Hospital in Los Angeles.

Football continued to modernize. The Colts and Rams game was played in Boston on a Saturday instead of Sunday in order to telecast it to 88 stations in 43 states. The game, which was blocked out locally, could be viewed by owners of video sets, who would drop two-bits into a coin attachment to see the game on a closed circuit. It was like an early pay per view. As many as 35,000 fans were expected to attend. But as much as the game was changing, segregation was still stringently enforced even in the NFL. Games in the south continued to be hard on the black players in the National Football League, players like George Taliaferro and Buddy Young, despite being two of the stars of the team. In fact, Taliaferro and other black members of the Colts were still unable to use the same hotel accommodations as the rest of the players. Taliaferro could not be complacent. As he had at Indiana University, he decided to do something about the widespread discrimination in the NFL.

Taliaferro first tried to reason with the Colts general manager to enlist his help. "Segregation is expensive," he stated simply to the Colts GM, appealing to his financial sense. Taliaferro tried to convince him to let managers of pro football teams in the south know that if they wanted professional football in their states, they were going to have to change the Jim Crow laws; otherwise the professional football teams in the north simply would stop coming to play them. This probably would have worked. But it required the cooperation of those in charge of the teams in the north, something Taliaferro could not count on to happen. When his general manager did not offer help, Taliaferro had to take matters into his own hands. For their next game in the south, the Colts traveled to Tulsa, Oklahoma. Taliaferro and six other black players stayed at a hotel owned by a black friend of his who had graduated from the School of Law at Indiana University. Normally he would have allowed the players a free stay at his hotel, but instead sent the Colts a bill for more than $300, a large sum for the 1950s. When Taliaferro's friend received the money from the Colts, he gave it back to the players who had stayed there. He had just wanted to help Taliaferro make the point that segregation was costly. It was a beginning, something that would hopefully get team managers talking about segregation. If people wouldn't look at it from a moral perspective, maybe the financial ramifications of the practice would be considered. At the very least, it was a place to start.

Taliaferro is still with the Colts in this 1954 Bowman football card. That season he was plagued by injuries.

GEORGE TALIAFERRO
BALTIMORE COLTS

Taliaferro, though sensitive to racial discrimination and active in changing society's boundaries, never became consumed by racism. His identity was not wrapped up in the color of his skin. He was a husband, father, and professional football player. The professional football player was the only identity that wouldn't last. This career was already coming to an end. Having had a good season despite a losing record, Taliaferro stayed with the Colts in 1954, the same year a new rule requiring all players to wear facemasks was adopted. The Colts had a new head coach, Weeb Ewbank, who immediately began working on building a winning football team. This period of time was still what Taliaferro refers to as B.U., Before Unitas, for the Colts, and Ewbank's success was not to come for a couple more years; by then, Taliaferro would no longer be with the franchise.

Ewbank had kinks to work out in his team before the Colts could become a success. Injuries were among these problems. Taliaferro had an impressive preseason showing. "Taliaferro is a key man in the Colts' plans for 1954. With four year[s] of NFL pro football behind him and a fine statistical record to boot there is no reason that 1954 cannot be his finest in the game," a Colts program said. That may have been true if it weren't for a series of injuries at the beginning of the season that plagued him for its entirety. He injured his hand and sprained his ankle early on, and at the end of the season he had to have cartilage removed from his right knee. The effect of the injuries was apparent in his personal statistics for the season. He played only three games and had negative 2 yards on three rushing attempts. He was held to just 457 yards for the season. The Colts, who had been hopeful about the Taliaferro/Young combination, ended the season with a disappointing three wins and nine losses, and for the first time in his professional career, Taliaferro was not on the Pro Bowl roster.

His statistics didn't keep him from playing another year. A Baltimore Colts news release in June of 1955 indicated that the Colts had signed Taliaferro to play again with the team. Taliaferro's injuries had healed, and he had been working out regularly during the winter and spring. Optimistically, the news release reported that the twenty-eight-year-old Taliaferro: "would report to camp in the best shape he has been in in several years." Doctor Dan Fortman, Taliaferro's new surgeon, was a former Chicago Bear lineman. He had Taliaferro exercising every day, and it looked like Taliaferro was going to make a comeback. He was expected to resume his punting duties, which had been covered by Cotton Davidson, who had left for the service. The reality of his situation was actually quite different. Unfortunately, Taliaferro's injuries had not healed as fully as had originally been anticipated, and he was unable to meet the expectations of his team. In the middle of the season, the Colts traded the injured Taliaferro to the Philadelphia Eagles. His family, whose house had been swallowed by the Santa Monica route of Los Angeles's new expressway system, had just moved to join him in Baltimore.

While Taliaferro was playing for the Colts and the Eagles, the Civil Rights Movement was gaining ground. The National Association for the Advancement of Colored People (NAACP), of which Taliaferro has been a lifetime member, had helped end school segregation by winning a court ruling on its unconstitutionality. While the courts had mandated that segregation was acceptable as long as schools were "separate and equal," the NAACP provided information showing that the amount of spending on white schools was nearly three times that of black schools, an average of $37.87 per pupil for white students compared to the $13.08 spent on black students. On May

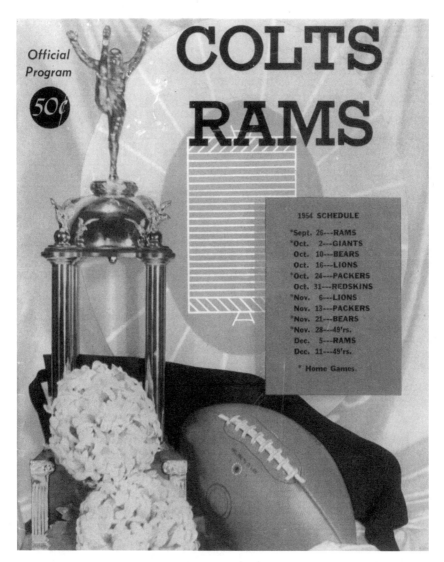

A football program from the Rams–Colts game in Baltimore on September 26, 1954.

17, 1954, the U.S. Supreme Court case of Brown v. the Board of Education of Topeka overturned Plessy v. Ferguson, the case that in 1896 had sanctioned racial segregation in public schools. In 1955 Rosa Parks was arrested for not giving up her seat to a white person on a bus, beginning the Montgomery Bus Boycott. Shortly after her arrest, Dr. Martin Luther King, Jr., was elected president of the Montgomery Improvement Association, making him the

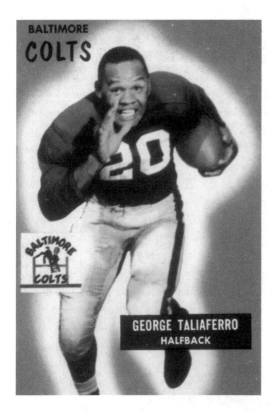

Taliaferro's last season of professional football. He is with the Colts for half of the season before he is traded to Philadelphia. This 1955 Bowman football card shows him still with the Colts.

boycott's spokesperson. Ultimately, the boycott led to an important 1956 Supreme Court ruling that deemed bus segregation illegal and set a precedent for desegregation.

These historic events affected the Taliaferro family, especially impacting Taliaferro's decision to stop playing professional football. The decision was a difficult one to make, but Taliaferro felt that it was the only real choice. He had always been the best conditioned athlete he could be so that he could give his best performance for his team. No longer able to do that, he decided it was time to retire. He also did not want to be remembered for playing what he referred to as "a poor brand of football." His pride and team loyalty were not his only considerations. The risk of exposing himself to further injury and ultimately doing more permanent damage to his already-injured knee also had to be considered. The birth of his third daughter, Donna, on November 20, was a reminder that even a bad football season couldn't keep him from the delight his growing family gave him.

His trailblazing football career, which included impressive statistics, was coming to an end. Taliaferro was one of the last professional football players to play both offense and defense. Today, Taliaferro says, a team would have to hire seven people to play the positions he did. He was a passer, runner, receiver, punter, punt returner, kick-off returner, and defensive halfback in the "Iron Man" days of football. Taliaferro finished his professional football career having been shuffled from one team to another, with never anything beyond a mediocre season. Despite his strong individual statistics and three Pro Bowl appearances, Taliaferro had never played for a winning football team in the National Football League. "I was never able to get on a club where I wasn't the whole offense," he said. The Colts, under the new leadership of Weeb Ewbank, ended up breaking the .500 mark for the first time in 1957 with Johnny Unitas leading the way. They actually won the NFL championship in 1958 and 1959. By that time, Taliaferro was no longer playing professional football.

Even though he had never played for a winning team, Taliaferro did not regret his decision to play for the Los Angeles Dons instead of the Chicago Bears. "I sometimes speculate I would have gotten greater press coverage, more money, and a stable career," he said. "Then I wonder about my social life and the opportunity to learn and grow by traveling and meeting new people and experiencing the changes brought on by being on my own far from Gary," he went on to say. There was no doubt that if Taliaferro had decided to realize his childhood dream and sign with the Bears, he would have played for a better football team under outstanding coaching. Still, Taliaferro said, "I was truly happy just to be playing professional football!"

For his career, Taliaferro had rushed for more than 2,200 yards in 436 attempts, caught 95 passes for 1,300 yards, returned 27 punts for 251 yards, and had another 2,000 yards in 67 kickoff returns. He also threw 248 passes with 92 completions for 10 touchdowns and 1,633 yards. Gill called him "in fact if not in reputation, the NFL's first black quarterback." More important than his personal statistics and the win/loss records of his various teams was Taliaferro's role in the NFL as a trailblazer. His status as the first African American drafted by an NFL team and as the first black quarterback may not have immediately opened doors for other black ball players, but it was a place to start. It was something.

Life after Football

Taliaferro's decision to retire from professional football was made easier for two reasons. First, he had already accomplished what he had wanted—to play professional football and have fun doing it. Second, Taliaferro had an education. This education, however, did not ensure the smooth transition from professional football that he had hoped. Unlike today's professional athletes, Taliaferro had not signed multi-million dollar contracts, did not have mega endorsement deals, and did not have a career in broadcasting to fall back on, so life after football was going to be more challenging than he had anticipated, and his skin color was making it more difficult.

"The American Dream was still eluding me because I was black," Taliaferro said. This was an obstacle that, up until this time, he had been able to manage. He had always fought it with some success. Upon retiring from the NFL, he returned to Baltimore with his family, where he found that racism was not always something he could overcome. There, he decided to pursue a job as a high school football coach. Degree in hand, he was determined to be like the man who had coached him in high school. He had always credited high school coach Bo Mallard with being a positive influence on his life and with teaching him everything he knew about football. Now he wanted to pass on what he had learned to other young football players.

The first obstacle to his plan was the public school system in Baltimore, which would only hire black teachers and coaches for one of its two all-black schools. There were no positions open in either one. This made Taliaferro's dream of becoming a role model a lot more difficult to achieve. Not new to obstacles, Taliaferro managed this one by contacting the dean of HPER at Indiana University and explaining the problem he was having with the Baltimore school system. "I am open to suggestions," he told the dean, who suggested Taliaferro pay a visit to Baltimore's Superintendent of Physical

Education, an Indiana University alum who might be able to help a fellow IU grad. To Taliaferro, this connection was promising.

With a renewed sense of confidence, he paid a visit to the superintendent's office. "I walked in with my little diploma in hand and my little dressed up self," Taliaferro said. He introduced himself to the superintendent and explained that he was also an Indiana University alumnus. He proceeded to explain his situation and told him about his conversation with the dean. The superintendent listened to Taliaferro, and then repeated what Taliaferro had already heard. "Well, we only have two high schools that are all-black, and those are the ones that you would qualify to teach at," was the curt reply. Once again Taliaferro was reminded that his skin color meant he was not entitled to something even if he worked hard and was qualified.

"I almost choked. I almost died. I'm sure I didn't hear much of what he said after that. I was so angry that here I had persevered to get this degree over a five year period . . . and then to have a man to tell me the only place I could work would be in a black school. I just couldn't believe it. I simply could not believe it. And so there I was with a family and now with no way to support my family," Taliaferro said. In an article by Chuck Crabb, an assistant in IU's Athletic Publicity Office, Taliaferro related the story: "One problem I had was I am Black. Before that time, I was able to surmount and hurdle this problem. The Baltimore area Black schools had sufficient staffs. There was no compelling rush to help George Taliaferro get a job."

Taliaferro was more angry and frustrated than he had been in a long time. Here he was, a man with professional football experience who had played in three Pro Bowls, and he wanted nothing more than to pass on this knowledge and experience to young Baltimore football players. How could they turn him down solely on the basis of his skin color? It was simply beyond Taliaferro's comprehension. In desperation, he went to some known gangsters and asked for work. He thought if he worked for them, he would be able to adequately provide for his family. The gangsters, who apparently recognized Taliaferro's inherent goodness, refused him a job.

"You're throwing your life away because you're angry," one of them told him, explaining why they wouldn't help him.

"I must do what I need to do to care for my family," Taliaferro insisted, growing angry. But his pleas fell on deaf ears, and he was sent away, still jobless.

He didn't tell Viola about that futile attempt, but she knew he was growing frustrated in his search to find employment. She continued to encourage him. "So you can't teach in Baltimore. So what, let's do something else," she said. Forced to pursue another way to support his family, Taliaferro took the only job he could find, selling cars, which turned out to be a better situation than he had anticipated. Because his name was so well known in Baltimore, the car business actually proved quite successful. It was based on commission and wasn't steady income, however, so he found other ways to supplement his income for those times when his checks were too paltry. He managed to do some substitute teaching in the two black high schools when he was not at the car dealership, and did a little golf hustling on the side. Golf had been a hobby of his for many years, likely because he was so good at it. He would find businessmen who had money but who couldn't match his golf skills, then he would take advantage of them by wagering on golf games between them.

Although this was providing the financial stability he desired for his family, Taliaferro could not be satisfied selling cars and golf hustling. He wanted to help people, and he didn't think his skin color should bar him from doing so. He finally decided, with encouragement from his wife, to pursue a degree in social work, a degree that would allow him, "to work with people, period." He had not given up on his dream of helping others the way his high school football coach had helped him, even if he couldn't teach. He was finally going to do something about it.

In 1957, Jackie Robinson retired from baseball, and Dr. King, who spoke to a crowd of 15,000 people in Washington, D.C., formed the Southern Christian Leadership Conference to fight segregation and obtain civil rights. This was also the year Taliaferro began working as director of the Lafayette Square Community Center in Baltimore while pursuing a master's degree in social work. He had found his purpose in life and a position that provided financial stability. While he still golfed on the side, now it was for enjoyment. Having almost let the anger and frustration of racism ruin his life by seeking employment with known gangsters, Taliaferro had learned a valuable lesson. "People who are winners are engaged in making things happen and do not have the time to be consumed with hatred or putting others down," he said. He was going to continue being one of the ones busy making things happen. At the community center, Taliaferro was the only paid staff member. He set up the program, taught volunteers, and raised funds. When he left, it took three people to replace him.

Taliaferro's community-mindedness was evident in his subsequent career choices as well. In 1959, while continuing to work on his degree, Taliaferro became a caseworker for the Prisoner Aid Association in Baltimore. He was also a psychiatric social worker at the Clifton T. Perkins Hospital and senior case worker at the Shaw Residence in Washington, D.C. These were paid positions, but also provided scholarships toward his degree. He continued to work with prisoners until 1964. In the Virginia penal system, Taliaferro saw people who reminded him of the person he was on the day he went to the gangsters. They were angry people who had let their anger and frustration dictate who they would be, people who had made the choice to become products of racism.

His own life turned out differently from theirs. On December 21, 1962, Taliaferro's youngest daughter, Terri, was born, the same year Taliaferro earned his master's degree from Howard University. With this degree, he had more than fulfilled the promise he made to his father. "You have what it takes to be anything you want to be if you are willing to make the sacrifice," Taliaferro said. He had learned that lesson through his own experiences. "Remember two things about me," Taliaferro said. "First, I am educated. Second, I am educated. In spite of all odds I have beat the system. I have four daughters and a wife who have beat the system. And I have seven grandchildren who are preparing to beat the system." Every day Taliaferro's mom and dad had said, "We love you. You must be educated." Taliaferro's own siblings took this to heart. His older brother James was the only one who didn't finish college and that was because of World War II. Taliaferro had learned to value education and passed this on to his own kids.

Becoming a social worker was just one way Taliaferro was helping others. He felt there were other ways he could help as well. While still living in Baltimore, he got involved in Big Brothers/Big Sisters. His first Little Brother was Clarence Clark. "CC" lived on an alley street in a row house downtown. There was no father in the home, but he lived with his mother and three sisters. CC, a thirteen-year-old seventh grader, had a juvenile record for missing school, shoplifting, and breaking and entering. He had been on the list for a Big Brother for a year. A caseworker introduced Taliaferro to him, and they made arrangements for Taliaferro to pick him up the following morning at 8:30. Excited at finally having a Big Brother, CC dressed in his nicest clothes for the meeting. But upon learning that CC had not seen grass because his entire neighborhood was concrete, Taliaferro decided they should spend the day outside. They found a change of clothes for CC and spent the day working outside together.

The next morning they met again. With his mother's permission, CC attended church with the Taliaferros, and then spent the remainder of the day at their house. They talked, ate, watched TV, and made plans for the following weekend. Those plans never happened. That Wednesday CC was caught in the warehouse two doors down from his home stealing 20 cartons of cigarettes and five hams. He was sent to the Youth Correctional Facility in Hagerstown, Maryland, for 18 months. Fortunately for him, this was during the time that Taliaferro was doing an internship with the institution as a graduate student at Howard University. They were able to continue their relationship while CC served his time there. When the 18 months had passed and CC returned home, they began regular weekly visits. Often they included the Taliaferros' daughters and CC's sisters in their outings, visiting parks and zoos, holding picnics, going to ball games, and finding quiet times to talk.

In May of 1963, following mass demonstrations against segregation that led to the arrest of Dr. Martin Luther King, Jr., for demonstrating without a permit, the Birmingham Truce Agreement was announced. Stores, restaurants, and schools were to be desegregated. That same year, 250,000 people attended Martin Luther King's Freedom Walk in Detroit, Michigan. The rights Taliaferro had been fighting for were finally becoming a reality throughout the country. The Taliaferros moved to Washington, D.C., in 1964, where he continued as a social worker, and carried on his work with the prison population at a halfway house for rehabilitating convicts. He also worked as a director of the Prince Georges County Community Action Programs for the United Planning Organization, a community outreach program aimed at providing services for the needy as well as developing job programs. At the same time, he served as executive director of a drug abuse counseling center. From 1966 to 1968 Taliaferro was an assistant professor at the University of Maryland Graduate School of Social Work. He also received a certificate in criminology from the University of Montreal, something he felt would help with his work in the penal system.

Taliaferro went back to Bloomington in 1967 for celebrations for the Indiana University football team, which had been selected to represent the Big Ten Conference in the 1968 Rose Bowl. He attended several parties and celebrations and visited old friends while he was in Indiana. At one point, he passed through Linton, Indiana, where he took down their welcome sign which he remembers said: "Black people—don't let the sun going down catch you in this town." He never stopped fighting discrimination. Nineteen forty-five teammate Howard Brown, who was still serving the Indiana football program as an assistant football coach, also attended the reunion. Although Taliaferro had re-established some of his Indiana University connections, it wasn't quite time for him to return to the Hoosier state. Nevertheless, each career move was bringing Taliaferro closer to Indiana.

For two years, from 1968 to 1970, Taliaferro was the vice president and general manager of Dico Corporation, a subsidiary of Martin-Marietta Corporation in Washington, D.C. The goal of the company was to integrate the seriously unemployable into the private sector. As manager, Taliaferro developed a rapport with local law enforcement and correctional agencies as well as other community members in order to meet that goal. In 1969, the 100th anniversary of college football, while he was with Dico, Taliaferro was honored by IU fans who selected him to the first team of the IU All-Time Football Team, reminding him of fond memories and important people in his life. Three members of the 1967 Rose Bowl team were named with him: Harry Gonso, John Isenbarger, and Jade Butcher.

Taliaferro became dean of students at Morgan State University in 1970, a job many would consider challenging when taking into account the activism so prevalent on university campuses at the time. In a Hammel article Taliaferro explained why he didn't find it difficult: "All you have to do is listen. . . . I can honestly see in these students the George Taliaferro of 25 years ago, and I'm just like everyone else. . . . We are supposed to learn from history, but the paradox has been that we do not. I have tried to make an effort to defy that paradox and show those students that I have learned something from being on this earth." Aside from his duties as a dean, Taliaferro was also an unpaid assistant football coach and he became, around this time, the first "Negro" vice president of the association of former players for the Baltimore Colts. In a 1971 golf tournament, Taliaferro was partnered with Jackie Robinson, Joe Louis, and the first African American golfer in the PGA, Clifford Brown, an elite group of trailblazers.

In 1972, Taliaferro was asked to come to Indiana University to serve as a special assistant to IU president John W. Ryan, an opportunity he credits Howard Brown with bringing about. As a student and athlete Taliaferro had experienced segregation, racism, and discrimination at Indiana University. Nearly 30 years later, Taliaferro was offered a position at Indiana University with an office just across from President Ryan. As Ryan's assistant, Taliaferro's primary responsibility was to develop an Affirmative Action plan that included all eight Indiana University campuses. Bringing him in as the Affirmative Action coordinator may have been prompted by campus events such as the 1969 boycott and an incident with a professor in 1972.

A Rose Bowl appearance in 1968 was Indiana University's first and only appearance in the coveted game. Coach John Pont's previous head coaching engagements, seven years at Miami of Ohio and two years at Yale, had earned him a 55-27-3 record. During the 1967 season, the Hoosiers lost only two games to Minnesota and Southern Cal. Similar to the storybook ending Taliaferro's team had earned with a win over Purdue to end the season, the 1967 team's Old Oaken Bucket win to end the season earned the Hoosiers a trip to Pasadena, California, for the Rose Bowl. Even the 14 to 3 Rose Bowl loss to USC, during which O. J. Simpson rushed for 128 yards and two touchdowns, was not altogether disappointing for IU. The appearance in Pasadena was an honor for a team that had fought all season through close games to eke out wins, earning them the nickname "Cardiac Kids." Hoosier fans were already looking ahead to a possible return to the Tournament of Roses following the 1969 season. It looked like a good possibility at the beginning of the season, if not for a boycott midseason and three subsequent losses that kept that dream from becoming a reality. Fourteen African American players decided midseason not to go to practice because of racial issues they wanted brought to the attention of Coach Pont, 1967's national Coach of the Year Award winner. Calvin Snowden, a defensive end on that Rose Bowl team, explained why they felt the need to take such action.

Indiana University, he said, was a microcosm of society, and like society, black people were still being treated as second-class citizens. In Indiana football that translated to doing things like stacking black players behind each other, so that they would be competing against each other for positions instead of starting in other positions. Snowden pointed to Cordell Gill as one example. Gill, he said, was a talented linebacker who should have been starting in that position. Instead, he was made a defensive end, a position which wasn't as suited for his 5'9", 230-pound body, and played behind Snowden. Black quarterbacks were changed to running backs, according to Snowden, in an effort to keep the black players from starting at too many positions. But stacking, he said, wasn't the only issue. By 1969 there were 20,000 students at Indiana University, and his roommate was black. "Get my inference?" he asked. "I was faceless," he continued. White students would talk to him or study with him in private, but they wouldn't go to dinner or lunch with him; on campus they wouldn't acknowledge him. The N-word was leveled at him on campus as well. He also pointed to the fact that black players had been instrumental in getting to the Rose Bowl but had not reaped the same rewards from it as the white players had, including postseason honors. Finally, there were comments that bothered him. One of the trainers, Snowden said, often made comments that offended the black players. He asked Snowden before the Rose Bowl game if he had been dating Caucasian girls. "I always see you with some bitch," he said.

Snowden replied, "If I called the woman you loved a bitch how would you feel about that?"

The trainer continued, ignoring the question, saying he didn't think the pro scouts watching Snowden would appreciate him dating white girls.

"I don't think the pros care who I date," Snowden replied.

"The reality was we were a commodity to be used," Snowden said. Issues like the ones he experienced had prompted the black players to boycott practice. The boycott forced Coach Pont to have a meeting with his coaches to discuss the situation. They then met with the players, who were given the option of returning to practice without penalty. Only four of the 14 returned. John Andrews, who went on to play for the Baltimore Colts, was one of them. One reason for returning to the team, he said, was that the black players had originally only agreed upon a one-week boycott. However, with the intrinsic atmosphere of student protests in the '60s, the boycott lasted longer than they had originally anticipated. Also, unlike some of those who weren't going back, Andrews was a starter. He was the only black starter on offense his junior year. That didn't mean he didn't understand why they were upset. Players who had been starting quarterbacks and running backs in high school, he said, were moved to defense when they came to Indiana University, and the black players on defense were stacked, as Snowden had indicated, increasing their frustration and hindering their desire to return to the team. Finally, most of the players not returning were seniors and would only be missing half a season. Andrews, on the other hand, was only a junior, which would have meant more of a sacrifice if he hadn't returned.

According to Andrews, Larry Highbaugh, a sophomore, was a non-senior who *had* made that sacrifice. This was probably because, unlike Andrews, Highbaugh was not starting. He was one of the players, Andrews said, who should have been starting as wide receiver, but who was moved to defense where he was stacked behind another player. Highbaugh also ran track for the Hoosiers where he clocked a 4.2 forty and once won three events at the Big Ten championships. Unlike some of the players who did not return to practice, Highbaugh went on to play professional football, starting in the Canadian Football League. The players who did not return to practice were dismissed from the team, which ended with a 4-6 losing record, a blow to IU athletics and to a football program that had once been ahead of its time in race relations. The entire incident probably made it difficult, Andrews said, to recruit talented players, especially black players, in the next few years.

The Rafalko incident also may have prompted the hiring of George Taliaferro as Ryan's assistant. A letter of complaint about Professor Stanley Rafalko stated: "In Doctor Rafalko's course (Anatomy of the Ear and Vocal Cords), he had no syllabus, no required texts; he made frequent derogatory remarks about the physically handicapped and racist remarks about people of color all over the world." The letter included a quote by Rafalko: "All colored people have overdeveloped buccinator muscles and enlarged lips, which is why colored children have difficulty articulating and trouble in speech therapy. And what's worse, they're colored." A group of students protested Rafalko's racism with a teach-in, but according to the letter, it wasn't until 200 black students assembled on President Ryan's lawn that something was done about the situation. The letter stated that the Rafalko case was just one of several incidents. Indiana University was experiencing the same problems with race relations that were being felt across the country, and as Ryan's assistant, Taliaferro's duties would include making strides toward bettering these relations.

The IU Affirmative Action Plan wasn't his only duty. He would also handle any special assignments from Ryan as well as the recruiting and counseling of minority students, among other things, in addition to holding the position of assistant professor in the Graduate School of Social Service. As coordinator of the Affirmative Action Plan, Taliaferro was to develop a program for all eight Indiana University campuses to discourage discrimination against minorities and women. As Ryan's assistant, Taliaferro's services could be used by any department at Indiana University, and he was pleased when the athletics department began using him in a small recruiting role.

Taliaferro chaired the Big Ten Advisory Committee at this time as well. The committee, made up of one black athlete from each school, made recommendations regarding athletes and academics in the Big Ten and in the NCAA. During this time, his football skills had not been forgotten, and Taliaferro was inducted into the Indiana Football Hall of Fame in 1976.

His athletic and Affirmative Action duties collided in 1978 when Taliaferro criticized football coach Lee Corso for not abiding by Affirmative Action laws in hiring a replacement for an assistant coach. In an *Indiana Daily Student* article by Jane Ransom, Taliaferro said he was angry that the university had not advertised nationally in publications chosen to reach minority applicants as the law required. Normally, Taliaferro attended every football game, but in the article he said: "I decided not to purchase season tickets. I do not wish to support anything or anybody that is not going to abide by the law." Coach Corso at first insisted he had advertised, but later said he couldn't remember. Athletic Director Paul Dietzel, however, said he had already advertised for the assistant position when they hired two other coaches four months earlier and that it was not necessary to repeat the advertising. He and Corso both felt that there wasn't time to do that; the assistant coach's departure had been sudden and spring training was beginning. This, however, was not to be the only conflict between Taliaferro and Corso.

While Taliaferro was kept active with his many duties as President Ryan's assistant, Mrs. Taliaferro was busy as well. In her spare time, not something a mother of four has in abundance, Viola Taliaferro took law classes at Indiana University. She came from a family that was community-minded. Her parents were concerned and involved with the community and were actively involved in making it better. "They made things happen," she said. She, too, wanted to be an active participant in the community. "We each have that responsibility to make a contribution in some way," she said. She added that everyone does this in a different way, but that each should give as much as possible in whatever that way is.

To do her part, she enrolled part time in the School of Law in 1974 and started full time in 1975. By 1977 Viola Taliaferro had a law degree. Upon finishing her degree, she took and passed the state bar exam and then began practicing law in a private practice. Continuing their pattern of success, George Taliaferro received a letter that left him dumbfounded. He was, the letter had said, one of 11 men to be inducted into the College Football Hall of Fame in 1981. There he joined the ranks of Coach Bo McMillin, who had been enshrined in 1951, and Pete Pihos, who had been enshrined in 1966. With Taliaferro on the list of inductees for 1981 was Navy quarterback Roger Staubach. Inductees to the Hall of Fame have to have an outstanding collegiate football record and must have continued to progress as contributing citizens. Taliaferro certainly had accomplished both. President Ryan and three other IU delegates attended the induction ceremony which took place at the Waldorf Astoria in New York. "You stand for everything that is good in the game," the congratulatory letter, which was signed by Executive Director James L. McDowell of the National Football Foundation, stated. According to a Hammel article in the Bloomington newspaper, Taliaferro said to his wife, "Isn't it ironic I would get an honor of this kind, for just having fun?"

Despite his success, however, there had been some tough times, and more were to come. A run-in with IU basketball coach Bob Knight the same year he was inducted into the Hall of Fame was one example. The Taliaferros had made a vow that they would make Bloomington a welcoming place for black athletes. As long as he could help it, he said, none would leave Memorial Stadium or Assembly Hall without someone to say "I'm glad you're

George Taliaferro stands as he is honored as an inductee in the College Football Hall of Fame in 1981. To his right is Navy quarterback Roger Staubach who was also being inducted. *Photo courtesy National Football Foundation's College Football Hall of Fame.*

here." Because of this, the Taliaferros became surrogate parents to some of the black athletes who came through Indiana University. In 1981, at the end of basketball season, they were invited by a couple of these players to an end-of-the-season party, which was being thrown by some of the parents. The Taliaferros went to Assembly Hall to wait for the players. They were standing at the edge of the basketball court near the dressing room, when suddenly, Taliaferro said, the door was flung open and Bob Knight yelled to him, "And I don't want to see your face at the parents' party."

Not one to back down from anything, despite Knight's infamous temper, Taliaferro replied, "You son of a bitch, you better be there 'cuz that's where I'm going!"

Mrs. Taliaferro managed to calm her husband down and talked him out of attending the party and confronting Knight. "Where do you think we're going?" she asked. "Do you have a son [on the team]?"

Still angry, he decided to tell President Ryan about what happened. "I will

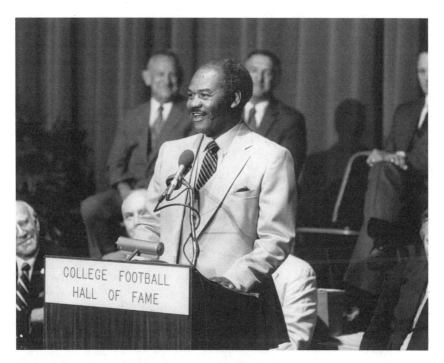

George Taliaferro addresses the audience at his induction into the College Football Hall of Fame. He had told his wife, Viola, "Isn't it ironic I would get an honor of this kind, just for having fun?" *Photo courtesy National Football Foundation's College Football Hall of Fame.*

knock him out if he ever points at me in public," Taliaferro informed Ryan. "You either get a new coach or a new assistant," he continued.

Ryan managed to calm down Taliaferro and convince him to stay, that he was too important to lose. Taliaferro would be with Ryan less than a year, however. Shortly after another run-in with Coach Corso, he resigned. In 1982, while still serving as assistant to President Ryan, Taliaferro again publicly criticized Corso. Ironically, when Corso was hired parallels were drawn between him and legendary Bo McMillin, Taliaferro's mentor. Both men had inherited a program that had been unsuccessful, and both had the determination to make changes. Taliaferro had been a member of the team Ryan put together in 1972 to hire a replacement for Coach John Pont who had resigned. The team had decided on Lee Corso. Ten years later, however, at a luncheon of the Downtown Evansville Quarterback Club, Taliaferro criticized Corso's coaching style and handling of players. He told the club that

Louisville, Corso's previous coaching engagement, had painted a favorable picture of him to Indiana's committee because they wanted to get rid of him. The story of Taliaferro's public criticism of Corso was all over the papers the next day. Although Taliaferro publicly apologized for anything that might have hurt the Corso family, he said he stood behind his remarks.

Apparently, there were some people who agreed. One Bloomington resident wrote a letter to the editor of the Bloomington *Herald-Times* in support of Taliaferro. He pointed to Corso's record, 36 wins, 2 ties, and 62 losses as reason enough for the remarks. Despite speculation by local reporters that he would be fired, Peter Fraenkel, another Ryan assistant, said that Taliaferro's comments would not endanger his job. Taliaferro, however, after implementing and overseeing the Affirmative Action programs at Indiana University for more than a decade, felt it was time to move on. He requested a change of positions at the university. There was some media speculation that the reassignment request was prompted by the public controversy that came after Taliaferro's criticism, but that was confirmed neither by the university nor by Taliaferro. Regardless, he was subsequently reassigned to the dean's office of the School of Social Work, where he would be an assistant to Beulah Compton, the school's acting dean.

From there, in a classroom in Ballantine Hall, Taliaferro began to teach social work theory and practice. He would stand at the front of his classroom a living, breathing example of what he taught. The man who taught his students that "every person has worth and dignity" taught them by example, by treating others that way. In 1991, I was one of those students. My roommate Lori had taken his class and kept telling me I just had to enroll. I was a secondary education major, but I needed another elective, so I signed up. I happened to be on crutches the first day of class, nothing major, just some cartilage problem with my knee, probably from playing softball and volleyball in high school. When I walked into the classroom for the first time, George Taliaferro greeted me with, "Well, there's One Hung Low!" He laughed and the lines around his eyes multiplied. It was an 8:00 AM class, and he had already managed to get a smile out of me, so that was something. One Hung Low remained my nickname for the duration of the semester. It didn't take long for me to figure out why my roommate had insisted on my taking the class.

There have been events in my life that I knew were turning points as they were happening. One of those moments was the day my grandmother said, "Don't let the anger get to you. If you leave it inside, it will eat away at you. You have to let it out." With that piece of advice my grandmother gave me a voice—she gave me power. Walking into George Taliaferro's class that first morning was another turning point. It didn't happen in one sudden realization like my grandmother's words; it was more of a gradual assimilation. With each new lesson, my eyes were opened wider. Taliaferro taught that everyone has worth and dignity. Everyone has a story, he told our class. His goal, he once said, was to meet someone new every day, to hear their story. The lessons continued. Learn from history, he urged us. Listen to the stories of others. Learn from others. Learn from your own experiences and pass those lessons on. While I became more aware of others around me, I began to see myself differently as well, as someone with worth and dignity, someone worthy of respect.

On exam days Taliaferro would hand out the blue books for taking essay tests that every college student dreads. After the exam he would write on the board, with the long, leathery fingers that had thrown and caught so many passes in the NFL, "All Sickness Ain't Death," the saying he had first heard from his construction boss, Jeter Means. He never explained. He just wrote it there for the class to figure out for themselves. We usually just laughed, equating it with the pressure those blue books could bring. We had no idea that the man standing in front of a classroom in Indiana University's Ballantine Hall had once experienced racism and segregation on that very same campus, that the life he lived was so symbolic of that saying.

Taliaferro reminded us to spell his name correctly on the blue book cover or he would not bother to grade the exam. When he said it, though the laugh lines would appear around his eyes again, we were never sure if he was joking. So we had all memorized the correct spelling and cautiously printed it on the cover of our blue books. I still don't know if he would have actually carried out the threat, but I do know the name is important to Taliaferro—it has a history, a story.

Taliaferro's great grandfather was a slave owned by an Italian physician with the surname Tagliaferro. The "g" is silent. On September 22, 1862, President Abraham Lincoln issued the Emancipation Proclamation, thus ending slavery and forever changing the life of Taliaferro's great grandfather. His owner told the former slave he could keep the surname if he wanted, even though he no longer belonged to him. Taliaferro's great grandfather kept the name, but he dropped the "g" to make it his own.

Over 100 years later, George Taliaferro, on an Alaskan cruise on a ship with an Italian crew learned that the name meant "iron worker," an appropriate name for a man who played seven positions in football during its Iron Man days and whose father had worked in a steel mill most of his life. Another anecdote regarding his name was told to him at an NFL outing long after he had retired from the sport. Ralph Guglielmi was a Notre Dame alum who was the 1955 MVP of the College All-Star game. He had since retired from the Washington Redskins and was attending the same NFL function as Taliaferro. Guglielmi said that his father, an Italian immigrant, would brag at the local barbershop about the great Italian kid at Indiana University, George Taliaferro. He went so far as to brag that he knew the family well, "a good Italian one." His constant bragging had even prompted one of the other regulars there to write to the university to get a picture for him. When the picture arrived, all the men in the barbershop were surprised to see the smiling face of George Taliaferro.

Taliaferro's name had a history, one that was a part of who he was. In a class about listening to the stories of others, it was important that we knew how to spell it, that we had listened, that we understood it was part of him. While he did tell us some stories about his name, he never mentioned his NFL career to his classes. It had nothing to do with what he was teaching, he explained. Instead, he taught us the Social Work Code of Ethics, that every person has worth and dignity. He always stressed the *every* part. The second was that "all human beings have the right to self determination." He wanted his students to see others differently, maybe see themselves differently as well. Understanding our place in the world and taking an active role in making it a better place was important to him. Upon entering the classroom one day we noticed that he had written on the board: "May our complacency disturb us profoundly today." He left it there for us to ponder. I have never forgotten it.

I always tried to avoid early morning classes when I registered, and on the occasions when I did end up in one, I would typically get up with 10 minutes to throw on a pair of sweats over my pajamas and haul myself to class. When it was over, I would peel off the sweats and head right back to bed. Later it would feel as if the class had just been a dream. This was not the case with Taliaferro's class. It was apparent to the students, who were more attentive than most early-morning participants, that even though we did not know about the arduous journey that brought Taliaferro to the classroom, he was not reading to us from a textbook. He seemed to embody what he taught. Or maybe it was just because if Taliaferro noticed anyone asleep he would whisper, "hip hip," the cue for the rest of the class to tiptoe to the culprit and yell "hooray!" At the end of class he'd say "Grab your hats," our cue to leave, but we were always surprised that it was already time to go.

Thinking his class should be required for every IU student, Lori and I ended up convincing our other roommate, Michelle, to take his class as well. When her semester was over, we decided to take him to dinner to thank him for everything he had done for us. We had all switched our majors to social work because of the profound influence he had on our lives. (I switched back to education, but my two roommates earned their social work degrees.) We decided to "break bread," as he put it, at Macri's Deli, my favorite Bloomington restaurant. When we arrived, three young white girls and one grandfatherly black man, the hostess approached.

"Will there be four of you?" she asked.

"Yes, I'm dining with my daughters," he replied.

She laughed.

"What? You don't think they can be my daughters?" Taliaferro asked. This time there were no laugh lines. He just said it, straight faced, serious.

She stammered. No actual words came out. The three of us just watched the whole thing, not giving it away, not laughing, just wondering what would happen next. The serious look didn't last long; the lines appeared around his eyes and he started to laugh. We started to laugh, too, but the waitress was still a little shocked. She finally forced a chuckle and showed us to our table, which happened to be next to a table with an army recruiter. Before we had even sat down, Taliaferro was trying to get the recruiter to take his "daughters" who needed some discipline, he said.

While Taliaferro was shaping future social workers, Mrs. Taliaferro was also making her mark on Bloomington. From 1989 to 1995, she worked as a magistrate. Then in 1995, Viola Taliaferro was appointed as a Monroe County Circuit Court Judge. She had raised four daughters, and was now influencing other young lives. As a juvenile court judge, she chose the best rehabilitation options for Monroe County's juvenile offenders. George Taliaferro provided the nicknames to go along with her title. He often referred to his wife, lovingly, as "The Judge" or "Her Ornery." "The Judge" retired in December of 2004, leaving a legacy. She had been named Bloomington's Woman of the Year for 1999 and had won the Book of Golden Deeds Award for 2001. She was also very involved in the community through organizations like the Human Rights Commission, the Bloomington Safe and Civil City Project, and the Boy Scouts, just to name a few. She served in organizations for juvenile justice and family issues at the local, state, and national levels. Her focus, in and out of the court room, was on children. There is even an annual award named after her, the Judge Viola J. Taliaferro Award, which is given out to Hoosiers who work on behalf of children.

George Taliaferro was inducted into the Indiana University Athletic Hall of Fame in November 1992, an honor he probably would have been given earlier had he not been ineligible because he was employed by the university. In 1995 he was elected to the NFL Players Association's retired players' steering committee, a nine-man policy committee that represented 2,500 former players. The three-year term he would serve on the committee was only one of many engagements for Taliaferro. More important, he was actively involved in charity and in giving to the community. Taliaferro has been actively involved in at least a dozen community organizations. He started the Monroe County chapter of Big Brothers/Big Sisters in Bloomington, Indiana, where he served as a Big Brother, as its president, and on its board of directors.

COTA, or Children's Organ Transplant Association, is another of Taliaferro's charities, one that has helped thousands of sick children. He has raised millions of dollars for the organization. He hosts an annual celebrity golf tournament and auction, and makes celebrity appearances to raise money for COTA. He holds the George Taliaferro Open in Bloomington each year. It includes a celebrity golf tournament and charity auction to raise money for COTA.

Above and beyond his special organizations, Taliaferro has affected his community in other ways. The way he has lived his life provides an example to others. He treats people with respect. He thinks it is important to remember people's names and to address them by name. "It makes people feel special," he said. An especially difficult task was to meet someone new every day—another of his personal efforts.

Even after retiring from Indiana University in 1992, Taliaferro continues to learn and to help others. He has influenced lives. There is a long list of people who credit Taliaferro for the positive role he has played in their lives. For example, Taliaferro never lost touch with Sydney Cummings, his Gary, Indiana, neighbor, who followed his hometown hero around Gary. When Taliaferro played football at IU, he was never too busy to write his young protégé and remind him to obey his parents and stay out of trouble. Cummings would go to the movies to see the highlight films of the IU football team "just to see Fat on the screen playing for Indiana," he said. And when Taliaferro played pro football, he sent tickets to Cummings. Cummings remembers Taliaferro even introducing him to Buddy Young at one of those games.

"Because of him, I went to school," Cummings said of his hero. Cummings, who received a master's degree from Indiana University, went on to teach in Gary, Indiana, where he, like Taliaferro, could inspire people. Taliaferro had a similar effect on CC, the boy from Baltimore who had been his first Little Brother. CC also ended up doing well in school and graduated from college. He got married, and had a steady job. He ended up joining Big Brothers/Big Sisters and had a Little Brother of his own. Another Gary youth who watched Taliaferro play football was Fred Williamson, who played football for Northwestern and went on to play professionally for the Kansas City Chiefs, after which he went into the film industry. Taliaferro saw him at a golf outing and Williamson told others around him that Taliaferro was "the man that was my inspiration to get out of Gary."

Taliaferro collects golf balls, but he does not hoard them. The Dayton Youth Golf Academy gives underprivileged kids the opportunity to play golf. Taliaferro has been sending golf balls to the organization for more than a decade. So far, he said, he has sent about 5,000 packages with a dozen golf balls each. One year he took seven sets of re-gripped and polished golf clubs and 215 packages of a dozen balls to the organization. Golf plays a huge role in Taliaferro's life, and he likes to share that joy with others.

New York Yanks teammate Sherman Howard said about Taliaferro, "Whatever he does he wants to be the best, and he instills that in others, too." Howard added that Taliaferro has integrity, that he is "a man of his word," something that no doubt would have pleased Taliaferro's father. In 1998, the Indiana University Athletic Department honored Taliaferro, awarding him the Clevenger Award, the prize given to a former IU athlete who has continued to serve the athletic department.

A Bloomington, Indiana, second-grader wrote to Taliaferro requesting that he come speak at his school. It was Black History Month and his teacher had assigned each child a famous black person to research. The boy was disappointed to be researching Isom Dart, a cowboy who got into a lot of trouble and then managed to turn his life around, only to be killed by a bounty hunter. He and his parents were unimpressed with the message of that particular story and requested that the teacher allow him to research someone of his own choosing. Despite their pleas, he was stuck researching Isom Dart, but he wrote a letter to Taliaferro anyway, and Taliaferro spoke at his school.

Recently, I followed suit and asked George Taliaferro to come speak during Black History Month to the students at Westfield High School, just north of Indianapolis, where I am a teacher. While some of his speech was about his role in black history, it went beyond that; his lectures usually do. He encouraged the students to *do something*—to find something they love and to do it. To be successful. Being a follower, he explained, doesn't work. He stressed the importance of not yielding to social pressure, of avoiding drinking or doing drugs. You can never be as good at being someone else as you can at being yourself, he explained. "I will do whatever it takes to be the best me I can be," he told them, then urged them to do the same. He explained the need for them to love themselves. He weighs nearly the same now as he did 60 years ago when he was a football player because he takes care of himself. "I'm not waiting on you to love me—I love me," he explained. Then, as he held up the "Colored" sign he had long ago taken from the Princess Theater, he talked to them about the danger of being complacent. When his presentation was over, he looked out at the sea of high school students and said, "If you need to, come stand on my shoulders because the sky won't be too far away, and the sky's the limit."

He hasn't stopped inspiring me either. As I was having a phone conversation with him one recent evening, my youngest daughter came in to say goodnight. She hugged and kissed me, and I told her I loved her. She went off to bed, and I apologized to him for the interruption, explaining I had to give goodnight hugs and kisses. That was all it took for him to launch into one of his lectures. "You and Jon have built a beautiful foundation for your kids," he told me. Then he reminded me, "You are not only Mom, you are a friend, someone they can always turn to." He didn't mean friend in the same way some people think they need to parent, by being one of the kids. He meant that the kids have to know that they can talk to us about anything, that there is nothing they can't discuss with us. He told me that I have to be available to talk to them at any time about any subject; "I will remind you as long as I live of that obligation," he said. George and Viola Taliaferro built a strong foundation for their family on love and communication, leading by example. Each of the three times my youngest interrupted me as I wrote this paragraph, I stopped and gave her hugs and kisses and told her I love her.

Taliaferro continues to inspire. That is why, on June 17, 2006, Indiana University honored him with a Distinguished Alumni Service Award. The program for the awards dinner read, "An inspiration to tens of thousands of young people, George Taliaferro has exhibited throughout his life the courage and determination that made him an All-American both on and off the gridiron. . . . For his stalwart advocacy of a level playing field, we proudly celebrate the life and work of George Taliaferro and bestow upon him the title of Distinguished Alumnus."

He isn't forgotten in Gary, Indiana, either. The city celebrated its centennial in 2006. As part of the celebration, a list was compiled of Gary's 15 greatest athletes, a difficult task in a city renowned for its athletics. Al Hamnik wrote the story for the *Northwest Indiana Times*. On the list was George Taliaferro, and he was in good company. Tom Harmon, who attended Michigan, was the nation's leading scorer in 1939 and Heisman winner of 1940. Harmon also appeared on the covers of both *Time* and *Life*. Boxing champion Tony Zakm, football great Alex Karras, and Olympians Charles Adkins, Lee Calhoun, and Willie Williams were also on the all-star list.

George Taliaferro spent a lifetime overcoming obstacles. His determination, athleticism, and positive attitude and the conviction that education is important enabled him to break color barriers as a student and athlete in Bloomington, Indiana, and later as a professional in athletics and beyond. As the first black man to be drafted by an NFL team and as the first black professional quarterback, he paved the way for those who would follow. As an educator and as a person, he continued to be an inspiration. Today, the African American athletes and coaches in the NFL can continue to look at his example as the league continues its integration. George Taliaferro is the embodiment of the statement he wrote on the board after every exam in his social work class: All Sickness Ain't Death.

Integration of the NFL

Indianapolis Colts coach Tony Dungy, one of six African American head coaches in the NFL as of 2005, acknowledges the role of George Taliaferro as a trailblazer in the league. In a 2004 interview, Dungy—a quarterback in his college days at Minnesota—said, "While growing up, it was important to see guys like George. It allowed you to dream that one day you could do it. Had I not had that example, I don't know that I would have persevered." As a pioneer in professional football, Taliaferro helped open doors for other black quarterbacks. These innovations, however, took years to become widely accepted.

Taliaferro had been a quarterback as early as 1949, and Willie Thrower had quarterbacked one game in 1953 for the Chicago Bears, completing three of eight passes. In 1955 it looked like the trend would continue with Charlie "Choo Choo" Brackins. According to an article by journalist Cliff Christl, Brackins was a successful black quarterback from all-black Prairie View A&M College in Texas, who at 6'2" and 220 pounds was the perfect size for a quarterback. Like Taliaferro, Brackins had a successful college career, starting all four years and playing positions on offense and defense. The Green Bay Packers drafted him in the sixteenth round of the 1955 draft, making him the third black man to quarterback in the NFL and the only black quarterback of 30 quarterbacks in the league in 1955. He also played in the positions of kickoff returner and receiver. However, despite his impressive college record, size, and versatility, Brackins did not end up staying with the Packers for very long. He played seven games and threw two incomplete passes before he was dismissed for a curfew violation, Christl wrote. He continued, "Whether Brackins was a victim of the times or a victim of his own indiscretions is open to debate." Taliaferro said, "As a black quarterback, if you didn't come in and win the Super Bowl you weren't staying." That, he said, is what happened to Willie Thrower. Whatever happened with Brackins, it would be more than a decade before there would be another black quarterback in the NFL.

In 1960, for example, Sandy Stephens, who was the first black All-American quarterback and who had led the University of Minnesota to a national championship, never quarterbacked in the NFL despite being a second-round draft pick of the Cleveland Browns and a first-round pick of the American Football League's New York Titans. The American Football League existed from 1960 through 1969, but like the AAFC, it merged with the NFL. Because these teams had indicated that they would change Stephens' position to a running back or defensive back, he decided to play in the Canadian Football League instead. There, the Montreal Alouettes gave him the opportunity to play the quarterback position.

Six more years would pass before a black quarterback was successful in the position. According to Bob Gill, Charlie Green played for the minor league Pasadena Pistols of the Texas Football League. In his first season with the Pistols, Green threw for 2,209 yards and 24 touchdowns. He was even more successful the following year with 3,133 yards and 35 touchdown passes. Green was on the all-league team both years. An injury kept him from playing much in 1968, the year Marlin Briscoe and Eldridge Dickey were starting their careers. Dickey was the first African American to be drafted by the AFL or NFL in the first round when he was chosen by the Oakland Raiders. A record-breaking quarterback at Tennessee State, it looked hopeful that he would become the first established black quarterback, but that did not pan out. The Raiders offered Dickey more money to switch to wide receiver and practice with the quarterbacks in training camp, where he hoped to earn a position as quarterback anyway. Although he made a strong showing during training, he was placed permanently at wide receiver.

At this same time University of Omaha quarterback Marlin Briscoe was making his mark on professional football. On October 6, 1968, Briscoe, whose nickname was "the magician" because of his ability to get away from defenders to make a play, made history as a Denver Bronco when he became the first black starting quarterback in a major sports league. Initially Briscoe was a defensive back, despite having an impressive tryout at quarterback. He was put in as quarterback the third game of the season after backup quarterback Joe Divito, who was in for injured first-string quarterback Steve Tensi, failed to make an impression. Briscoe managed to impress the coaches, almost pulling off a win despite a 13-point deficit, thus earning the starting quarterback position. According to a College Football Hall of Fame article, at first he was concerned that his primarily white offensive line, many of whom were from the south, wouldn't block for him. But they did, and Briscoe started in seven games and set a Broncos record of 1,589 yards passing, 14 touchdowns, and 308 yards rushing. At the time, the Broncos belonged to the AFL, which was considered the more tolerant league of the two. Briscoe's impact, while a sign of progress, still did not make for an immediate change. The following year, despite his record-setting season, Briscoe was traded to Buffalo, where he was once again moved from quarterback to wide receiver. Professional football, it seems, would take one step backward for every step forward.

This frustrated Taliaferro. While serving as vice president of the Association of Former Colts Players, Taliaferro said he did not think there would be an African American quarterback or coach in the NFL during his lifetime. Despite his own trailblazing, integration was happening only gradually. Before the 1969 draft, James "Shack" Harris, who had set records as a starting quarterback at Grambling University, decided he would not be among those who had to switch positions in the pro arena. Like Taliaferro, he was frustrated by the attempts to keep black players from playing leadership positions in the NFL. He made it clear that he did not want to switch positions and that he did not want to be drafted by any teams looking to do so. In the College Football Hall of Fame article he said, "It was totally unrealistic to think you had a chance to play. There were all kinds of reasons why blacks weren't playing quarterback, saying we weren't smart enough or we ran too much, or we couldn't read a defense. . . ." While it was a risk to be so adamant, something which could have kept him out of professional football altogether, Harris ended up being drafted by the Buffalo Bills in the eighth round as a quarterback. Ironically, it was the Bills that had previously switched Briscoe to wide receiver. Harris attracted national attention when he started the opening game in the quarterback position. Unlike the black quarterbacks before him, Harris became the first established black quarterback in NFL history. Despite periods in which he was plagued by injuries and benched, Harris was a successful quarterback for most of his career, until his retirement in 1980.

By 1974, Joe "Jefferson Street" Gilliam, Jr., another Tennessee State University product, proved Taliaferro's prediction wrong again when he quarterbacked for the Pittsburgh Steelers. Gilliam—whose father was on the 1945 championship Indiana team with Taliaferro—was picked by the Steelers in the eleventh round of the 1972 draft. A players strike led to Gilliam's starting position. In 1974, quarterback Terry Bradshaw went on strike with other players, leaving the position open for Gilliam. He continued as the starter even after the strike, but when he stopped performing, Bradshaw stepped back in and led the team to a Super Bowl championship. Gilliam's success was short-lived and, like Harris, it wasn't enough to completely integrate the position. Gilliam died at age 49, having struggled with drug problems that kept him from getting his career back together.

Thus, even in the mid-1970s, after the Civil Rights Movement had been in full swing for some time, the African American quarterback was a rarity in professional football. According to a *Los Angeles Times* article by Robyn Norwood, this is because mainstream society was just not comfortable with African Americans as leaders, and the quarterback position was the key leadership position on the field. "The white-dominated football hierarchy often labeled blacks as 'athletes' who should play cornerback, receiver, or running back, sometimes suggesting that they lacked the passing and cognitive abilities to play quarterback," Norwood wrote.

Tony Dungy said this change may have been slow "because of people's perceptions of what that [the quarterback position] is and what it should look like." It takes a while, he said, to break through those preconceived ideas. African American quarterbacks, Dungy pointed out, were still a novelty even in college football in the 1960s. When he played college football in 1973, it was fairly well accepted in the Big Ten, but not nationally. That is one of the reasons, he said, for his decision to attend Minnesota. In 1977, when Dungy turned pro, there were not many black quarterbacks in the league. He was another example of one whose success at the quarterback position in college did not equate to playing the position professionally. Instead, he played defensive back.

In the late 1980s, Doug Williams of the Washington Redskins became the only African American quarterback to lead his team to a Super Bowl victory. Williams' life had been a series of firsts. At Grambling University, the same historically black college that had produced James Harris, he became the first black quarterback from a predominantly black school to be named to the Associated Press All-America team. He also became the first black quarterback chosen in the first round of the NFL draft when the Tampa Bay Buccaneers picked him seventeeth in the 1978 draft, and he was not asked to switch from the quarterback position to other positions, unlike many of the black quarterbacks before him. However, like his predecessors, Williams received taunting from some white fans which heated up when he was blamed by fans for the inability of his team to make it past Dallas in the playoffs. His volatile relationship with both fans and team owners eventually led to his decision to play for the rival league USFL, which folded almost as quickly as it started. His outspoken manner kept him from returning to the NFL, so he started coaching receivers at Southern University. Williams had resigned himself to that role when he was contacted in 1987 by the Redskins who wanted him as a backup quarterback. When Joe Schroeder struggled with injuries, Williams was put in as the starting quarterback during the playoffs. Under his leadership, the Redskins made it to the Super Bowl, adding another first to his list, becoming the first black quarterback to start in the Super Bowl. He went on to add yet another first as he led his team to a 42 to 20 win, winning the Super Bowl and then being named MVP. Even after his Super Bowl success, however, his career was not without problems. A couple of years after the win he was out of the NFL again, and while he had managed to blaze a trail as a black quarterback, it still was not generally accepted in the league.

At the same time as Williams, Warren Moon was asserting himself as a black professional quarterback. Although he had performed admirably at the position at his southern California high school, he was unable to interest the bigger universities in playing him. Instead, he attended Pasadena Junior College, where he was able to prove himself worthy of a position and earned the attention of Washington, which, unlike USC and UCLA, was offering him a scholarship to play as quarterback. Washington made the right decision. Moon led them to a 1978 Rose Bowl victory. Despite a successful career at Washington, however, Moon wasn't drafted in 1978, so he decided to play in the Canadian Football League, where he remained, racking up more than 21,000 passing yards, and leading the Edmonton Eskimos to five titles in his six seasons in the league. These numbers gained the attention of the Houston Oilers, who signed him in 1984. The Oilers were in the playoffs with Moon at the helm for the following seven years, after which he played for other NFL teams, not retiring until 2000. He finished his career with impressive statistics, never having the lackluster seasons other black quarterbacks had sometimes experienced.

Randall Cunningham was also making his way as a black quarterback at this time. Like Moon, the bigger colleges who were interested in him wanted Cunningham to switch positions. The University of Nevada Las Vegas (UNLV), however, would give him the opportunity to play quarterback, so his decision was an easy one. Impressive statistics at UNLV earned Cunningham a look from the Philadelphia Eagles who picked him in the second round of the 1985 draft. It took a couple of years, but Cunningham was the starting quarterback for the Eagles by 1987, and by 1989 he was one of the NFL's highest paid players. Cunningham had a few seasons that were a struggle, but his career, which spanned 16 years, had been for the most part a very impressive one.

Although things had started to change by the time Moon and Cunningham retired, in 1992 they were among just five black quarterbacks in the league, along with Jeff Blake, Rodney Peete, and Vince Evans. Throughout the decade, however, this started to change. Kordell Stewart was one reason. He was the second-round draft pick-up by the Pittsburgh Steelers in 1994. He played wide receiver and running back as well as quarterback occasionally, although he wasn't the starter. Steve McNair continued the trend by being drafted by the Titans in the first round of the 1995 draft. He became the second black quarterback to lead his team in a Super Bowl when the Titans lost to the Rams in the 1999 Super Bowl. In 1998 the 10 black quarterbacks on NFL rosters added up to more than there had been at any other time in NFL history, according to journalist Cliff Christl. While only four of them were starters at the beginning of the season, three others were starting by the season's end. Change was even more noticeable in 1999, when Daunte Culpepper and Donovan McNabb were selected in the first round of the draft. In 2000, John Posey wrote that the press had nicknamed the season "Year of the Black Quarterback." By this time, five of the 12 starting quarterbacks in the playoffs were African American and at least 14 had started at least one game during the season, according to Norwood. The 2001 draft further indicated that things had changed when Michael Vick was selected as the number one overall pick by the Atlanta Falcons. In 2005 a Vick/McNabb title game marked the first time that two black quarterbacks had started against each other in a conference championship.

The strides in integrating the quarterback position took decades, but the quarterback position was not the only one to integrate too slowly. Although African American players, including quarterbacks, now star throughout the NFL, black coaches are still a minority. The next step toward integration is for more minorities to get opportunities to coach, Dungy said. Lenny Moore, a Hall-of-Famer who holds the record for 18 consecutive games scoring a touchdown (Baltimore Colts 1963–1965), agreed in a 2002 *USA Today* article. In the piece, Moore indicated he was disappointed in the lack of black head coaches in the NFL. He referred to individuals from his era, "a lot of good folks with great minds, going down the drain," who would have made good head coaches, but who were unable to do so because of their color. Among them was George Taliaferro. Taliaferro knew that despite his hard work, he could not have a career in coaching. During his football career he didn't know any African American coaches, in college or pro football. Instead, he decided to get into social work so he could "help people from the cradle to the grave."

In 1980, there were 14 African American assistant coaches in the NFL, but by 1997, there were 103. By 2003, 154 of 547 assistants were black. The NFL is moving in the right direction, even if it is only plodding. In 2003, there were only three African American head coaches in the league, but by 2006 there were six. According to Frank Woschitz, director of the NFL Players Association, 50 to 60 black assistant coaches attend a training camp put on by the NFL each year, so maybe that number will continue to go up.

Super Bowl XLI—which was played on February 4, 2007, and pitted Lovie Smith's Chicago Bears against Tony Dungy's Indianapolis Colts—was the first time an African American head coach coached a team in the Super Bowl, only it wasn't one African American head coach, it was two. The Colts' victory ensured Dungy's place in history as the first black head coach to win a Super Bowl. Maybe just as significant as the fact that these two men continued making important strides in the integration of professional football is the fact that they are classy human beings whose examples will reach beyond fighting racism. Interestingly, it was the Chicago Bears that drafted Taliaferro, making him the first black man drafted by the NFL, and his trailblazing continued when he played for the Baltimore Colts.

Although George Taliaferro's contributions as the first black professional quarterback and as the first black man drafted by the NFL did not have an immediate effect on the league's integration, it was a valuable start. Taliaferro and other pioneers in the integration of the NFL represented hope and inspiration to others who followed. To Taliaferro, though, football was mainly about doing what he loved to do. He said, "Nobody ever enjoyed playing football any more than I did. I lived to play football; it was that much fun."

BIBLIOGRAPHY

AAC. 1949. "Life Short, But Turbulent: Competition Was Healthy for Pro Football." *Chicago Daily Tribune*. 10 December. ProQuest Historical Newspapers Chicago Tribune (1849–1985).

AcePilots. 2006. "The Tuskegee Airmen 332nd Fighter Group." http://www.acepilots .com/usaaf_tusk.html. Accessed 12 January 2003.

Adams, Lehman. 2004. Phone interview by author. 16 June.

Andrews, John. 2006. Phone interview by author. 20 July.

Arnold, Robert D. 1996. *Hoosier Autumn*. Indianapolis: Guild Press of Indiana.

Banks, Calvin. 2004. Phone interview by author. 16 June.

Banks, Sam. 1953. "George Is Real George." *Our Sports*. October/November, 20–21, 52–53.

Baumgartner, Jim. 2006. Phone interview by author. 28 December.

Bell, Jarrett. 2002. "'Circus' Acts Mock the Game." *USA Today*. 24 October.

"Bo McMillin Wins Big Ten Title: After 46 Years of Trying, Indiana Finally Wins Football Championship." 1945. *Life*. 10 December, 42–52.

Bolding, Mark. 2006. "The Chicago Charities College All-Star Game 1934–1976: The Night the Stars Came Out." 8 August. http://www.mmbolding.com/BSR/The%20 Chicago%All-Star%20Game_1949.htm.

Brown, Jeff. 1997. "Re-integration of NFL is focus of black athlete lecture." 20 February. http://dmolemiss.edu/archives/97/9702/970220/970220N4nfl.html. Accessed 21 October 2003.

Brown, T. J. 1997. "IU, Wells Played Role in Sports Integration, Too." *Indiana Daily Student*. 15 April.

Christl, Cliff. 1998. "Black QBs find more opportunities." *Journal Sentinel* Online. 8 November. http://www.jsonline.com/packer/sbxxxiii/news/qb110898.asp.

College Football Hall of Fame. 2006. http://cbs.sportsline.com/collegefootball/ story/2542579.

Cook, Bob. 1995. *Finally, Bob Cook Book on Bo McMillin*. Bloomington: Indiana University Varsity Club.

Crabb, Chuck. n.d. "George Is Home And He Loves It Here." Athletic Publicity Office, Indiana University.

Cromie, Robert. 1949a. "Hornets and Dons Renew an Old Feud." *Chicago Daily Tribune*. 27 October. ProQuest Historical Newspapers Chicago Tribune (1849–1985).

———. 1949b. "Hornets to Battle Dons Tonight: Los Angeles Must Win for Play-Off Bid." *Chicago Daily Tribune*. 28 October. ProQuest Historical Newspapers Chicago Tribune (1849–1985).

———. 1949c. "Hornets Beaten By Dons, 24–14: Coast Eleven Keeps Alive Play-Off Hope—Taliaferro's Passes Bring Victory." *Chicago Daily Tribune*. 29 October. ProQuest Historical Newspapers Chicago Tribune (1849–1985).

Cummings, Sidney. 2004. Phone interview by author. 28 March.

Drummond, Herbert. 2004. Phone interview by author. 15 June.

Dungy, Tony. 2003. Phone interview by author. 5 November.

Fullerton, Hugh, Jr. 1948a. "Pro Grid Peace Meeting Today." *Gary-Post Tribune*. 20 December.

———. 1948b. "Both Loops to Hold Player Drafts Today." *Indianapolis Star*. 21 December.

"Gary, IN." 2005. Encyclopedia of Chicago. http://www.encyclopedia.chicagohistory .org/pages/503.html. Accessed 30 August 2005.

"George Taliaferro Is 'Drafted' By Chicago Bears." 1949. *Chicago Defender*. 1 January. ProQuest Historical Newspapers Chicago Defender (1905–1975).

George Taliaferro statistics. http://www.pro-football-reference.com/players/ TaliGe00.htm. Accessed 5 June 2003.

Gill, Bob. 2002. "Five Forgotten Trailblazers." *Coffin Corner* 24, no. 6, 10–11.

Graham, Tom, and Rachel Graham Cody. 2006. *Getting Open: The Unknown Story of Bill Garrett and the Integration of College Basketball*. New York: Atria Books.

Grosshandler, Stan. 1982. "A Disgrace." *The Coffin Corner* 9. Professional Football Researchers Association-Pro Football History. http://www.footballresearch.com/ articles/frpage.cfm?topic-dallas52. Accessed 6 June 2003.

Hackett, David. 1982. "Taliaferro Full of Memories." *Indiana Daily Student*. 14 October.

"Hall of Fame—1992 Inductees." 2003. http://iuhoosiers.com/tradition/halloffame/ halloffame1992.html. Accessed 5 June 2003.

Halsell Gilliam, Frances V. *A Time To Speak: A Brief History of the Afro-Americans of Bloomington, Indiana 1865–1965*. Bloomington, Ind.: Pinus Strobus.

Hammel, Bob. 1981. "Taliaferro Joins College Football Hall of Fame." *Herald Telephone*. 8 December, p. 9.

———. 1995. "IU Stops Michigan in Opener." *Herald-Times*. 22 September, B1.

———. n.d. "All You Have to Do Is Listen—Ryan Aide Taliaferro." Indiana University archives.

Hammel, Bob, and Kit Klingelhoffer. 1999. *Glory of Old IU: 100 Years of Indiana Athletics*. Champaign, Ill.: Sports Publishing.

Hamnik, Al. 1993. "Taliaferro Continues His Battle." *Gary Post-Tribune*. 20 January.

———. 2006. "Gary's Top 15 Athletes Sure To Create Interest." *Northwest Indiana Times*. 6 July.

Horrigan, Joe. 1985. "Belly Up in Dallas." *The Coffin Corner* 2. Professional Football Researchers Association Pro Football History.

Howard, Sherman. 2003. Phone interview by author. 15 September.

Indiana Humanities Council. "This Far by Faith," part 8. www.ihc4u.org/thisfar8 .htm. Accessed 5 June 2003.

Indiana University. "Alma Pater: Herman B Wells and the Rise of Indiana University." http://www.indiana.edu/~libarch/Wells/wellsbio.html. Accessed 12 January 2003.

Indiana University Athletics. www.iuhoosiers.com/football/history. Accessed 20 June 2005.

Kennedy, Tom. 1944. "Taliaferro Tallies Twice as Roosevelt Beats S.B.C." *Gary Post-Tribune.* 2 November.

Kish, Bernie. 2003. Interview by author. 27 June. Tape recording, College Football Hall of Fame, South Bend, Ind.

Kutch, Joe. 1944. "No Foolin', Panthers Trip Rough Riders, 13-9." *Gary Post-Tribune.* 7 October.

Lewis, Carl. 1947. "The Old Bucket, Coveted Football Trophy, Speaks." *Indiana Daily Student.* 22 November.

Long, Howie, with John Czarnecki. 2003. *Football for Dummies, 2d ed.* Indianapolis: Wiley.

McIver, Stuart. 1954. "Pro Football Club History #11 The Baltimore Colts." *Sport.* December.

Michelson, Herb. 1952. "Campus Mourns Passing of Bo." *Indiana Daily Student.* 1 April.

Montieth, Mark. 1995. "Indiana's Best Football Season Ever." *Indianapolis Star.* 6 October, E1.

National Football League. Circa 1972. *The NFL's Official Encyclopedic History of Professional Football.* New York: Macmillan.

Nicholls, Shawn. 2003. The Rise of Black Quarterbacks. *Sports Illustrated for Kids.* 1 September.

Norwood, Robyn. 2000. "Black Quarterbacks Scoring in the NFL." *Los Angeles Times.* 30 December, D10.

Overmyer, Jack. 2005. Interview by author. 30 December.

Peterson, Robert W. 1997. *Pigskin: The Early Years of Pro Football.* New York: Oxford University Press.

Pimlott, Ben. 1996. "It's All in the Life." *New Statesman.* 6 November.

Posey, John. 2000. "Black Quarterbacks in Vogue in the NFL." http://www.blackathlete .com/nf1128.htm. Accessed 21 October 2003.

Prell, Edward. 1948a. "Bonuses Cause Headaches for Club Owners." *Chicago Daily Tribune.* 4 April. ProQuest Historical Newspapers Chicago Tribune (1849–1985).

———. 1948b. "2 Football Leagues Hurt By Cash War Several Teams Hit Hard."

Chicago Daily Tribune. 1 November. ProQuest Historical Newspapers Chicago Tribune (1849–1985).

———. 1949a. "All-America Will Continue—Lindheimer." *Chicago Daily Tribune.* 20 January. ProQuest Historical Newspapers Chicago Tribune (1849–1985).

———. 1949b. "All-America to Operate with Seven Teams." *Chicago Daily Tribune.* 22 January. ProQuest Historical Newspapers Chicago Tribune (1849–1985).

Pro Football Hall of Fame. "History." http://www.profootballhof.com/history. Accessed 20 October 2003.

"Pro Leagues Merge; End 4 Year Fight." 1949. *Chicago Daily Tribune.* 10 December. ProQuest Historical Newspapers Chicago Tribune (1849–1985).

Rampersad, Arnold. 1997. *Jackie Robinson: A Biography.* New York: Alfred A. Knopf.

Ransom, Jane. 1978. "Ryan Aide Faults Sports Hiring." *Indiana Daily Student.* 31 March.

Robinson, Rachel. 1996. *Jackie Robinson: An Intimate Portrait.* New York: Harry N. Abrams.

Schurz, John. 1995. "Alumni Enjoy True Homecoming." *Herald-Times.* 8 October, A1.

Sheer, Harry. 1949. "Pro Grid Player War Rages On. A.A. Leads Bidding for Stars." *Chicago Daily News.* 4 January.

Shub, Seymour. 1949a. "Not Upset over Dons Signing Taliaferro—Halas Eyes Pact with '2nd Bronko.'" *Chicago Sun Times.* 3 January.

———. 1949b. "Bears Hold NFL Draft Rights—Dons Ink Taliaferro but Halas Not Upset." *Chicago Sun Times.* 3 January.

Simpson, Isabella. 1984. "Scoop." *Steel Shavings: Sports in the Calumet Region* 10, 24.

Snowden, Calvin. 2005. Phone interview by author. 20 June.

Steers, Ed. 2005. Phone interview by author. 22 August.

Taliaferro, George. 1996. Interview by author. 30 September. Tape recording, Bloomington, Ind.

———. 2003a. Interview by author. 27 June. Tape recording, College Football Hall of Fame, South Bend, Ind.

———. 2003b. Interview by author. 16 July Tape recording, Bloomington, Ind.

———. 2003c. Interview by author. 22 July. Bloomington, Ind.

———. 2005a. Phone interview by author. 20 June.

———. 2005b. "I Didn't Do It." *Coffin Corner* 27, no. 5.

———. 2006a. Phone interview by author. 27 June.

———. 2006b. Phone interview by author. 14 July.

"Taliaferro of Indiana Signed for '49 by Dons." 1949. *Chicago Daily Tribune.* 3 January. ProQuest Historical Newspapers Chicago Tribune (1849–1985).

"Taliaferro Signs Contract with Dons." 1949. *Chicago Defender.* 8 January. ProQuest Historical Newspapers Chicago Defender (1905–1975).

Taliaferro, Viola. 2004. Interview by author. 29 June. Bloomington, Ind.

Teuuws, Len. 2003. Phone interview by author. 3 November.

University of Illinois. 1967. Sports Interviews. General Publications.

University of Notre Dame Official Athletic Site. 2006. "The Four Horsemen." http://und.cstv.com/trads/horse.html. Accessed 10 August 2006.

Vance, Lloyd. 2005. "The Complete History of African American Quarterbacks in the NFL." Black Athlete Sports Network. 29 August. http://www.blackathlete.net/artman/publish/article_01018.shtml. Accessed 2 December 2005.

Walsh, Steve. "Social Change Plays Out on Front Page." *Gary Post-Tribune.* http://www.post-trib.com/news/race1229a.html. Accessed 30 August 2005.

Warren, Harry. 1948. "N.F.L. Ends Conference with Draft." *Chicago Daily Tribune.* 22 December. ProQuest Historical Newspapers Chicago Tribune (1849–1985).

Werry, Norman S. 1944. "Fumbles Rule as Roosevelt Gets 7-0 Win Off Froebel." *Gary Post-Tribune.* 20 October.

———. 1944. "Moleskin Musings." *Gary Post-Tribune.* 12 September–25 November.

———. 1944. "Taliaferro's Touchdowns Beat Blue Raiders, 19-6." *Gary Post-Tribune.* 10 November.

Whicker, Mike. 1948. "The Birth of a Juggernaut." Reitz Football History, October. http://www.reitzfootball.com/lgs/19481001.htm. Accessed 18 October 2003.

Whirty, Ryan. 2002. "A Hoosier Trailblazer: Taliaferro Overcomes Obstacles to Excel at IU, in Professional Ranks." *Inside Indiana* 12, no. 9. 9 November.

———. 2003. "Making a Difference: Count to 30." Indiana University Alumni Association, March/April. http://www.slis.indiana.edu/news/story.php?story_id=608. Accessed 6 June 2003.

Woschitz, Frank. 2003. Phone interview by author. 4 November.

"Yankees Halt Rally by Dons to Win, 17-16." 1949. *Chicago Daily Tribune.* 25 November. ProQuest Historical Newspapers Chicago Tribune (1849–1985).

Ziegler, Valerie H. n.d. "C6–H0: The Centre Harvard Game of 1921."

INDEX

Page numbers in italics indicate illustrations.

Blanda, George, 117. *See also* Chicago Bears

Bloomington, Indiana, 2, 10, 15, 19, 20, 28, 56, 117, 153, 157; segregation in, 21, 28, 29, 33, 34, 35, 85–87, 100, 101. *See also* Indiana University, segregation

Boston Yanks, 38

Boyd, Bob, 119. *See also* Los Angeles Rams

Brackins, Charlie (Choo Choo), 158, 159. *See also* Green Bay Packers, integration of professional football

Bradshaw, Terry, 160, 161. *See also* Joe Gilliam, Pittsburgh Steelers

Briscoe, Marlin, 159, 160. *See also* Denver Broncos, integration of professional football, University of Omaha

Brooklyn Dodgers, 77, 81. S*ee also* All-America Football Conference

Brooklyn Tigers, 38

Brown, Clifford, 143

Brown, Howard, 30, 38, 42, 43, 53, 57, 142, 143. S*ee also* Indiana University

Buckner, Bill, 37. *See also* Indiana University

Buckner, Quinn, 37. *See also* Indiana University

Buffalo Bills, 160. *See also* American Football League

Buffalo Bisons, 77, 109. *See also* All-America Football Conference

Butler, Sol, 79. *See also* integration of professional football

Calhoun, Lee, 157. *See also* Gary, Indiana

Canadian Football League: Toronto Argonauts, 119; Winnipeg Blue Bombers, 119; Edmonton Eskimos, 162, Lenny Highbaugh, 145 (*see also under* Indiana University); Warren

Moon, 162, Sandy Stephens, 159

Cannady, John, 42, 53, 57. *See also* Indiana University

Canton Bulldogs, 79, 81. *See also* Gideon Smith

Carmichael, Hoagy, 56. *See also* Bloomington, Indiana

Carr, Joe, 101. *See also* National Football League

Centre College, 25, 51. *See also* Harvard College, Bo McMillin

CFL. *See* Canadian Football League

Chicago Bears, 3, 102–104, 117, 118, 128, 134, 137, 158, 164. *See also* George Blanda, Chicago Cubs, Dan Fortman, George Halas, Lovie Smith, A.E. Staley

Chicago Black Hawks, 81. *See also* integration of professional football

Chicago Cardinals, 109. *See also* National Football League

Chicago Cubs, 103. *See also* Chicago Bears

Chicago Hornets, 108. S*ee also* All-America Football Conference

Chicago Rockets, 77. S*ee also* All-America Football Conference

Children's Organ Transplant Association, 154

Chimes, George, 61. *See also* University of Michigan

Cleveland Browns, 77, 82, 106, 108, 109, 110, 159. *See also* All-America Football Conference, Marion Motley, Bill Willis

Cleveland Rams, 38, 82. *See also* Los Angeles Rams

Coffee, J.C., 14, 15, 22. *See also* Indiana University

College All-Star Game, 100, 105. *See also* Pete Pihos, Philadelphia Eagles, Buddy Young

College Football Hall of Fame, *xiv,* *43,* 68, 147, *148, 149. See also* John Green, Bo McMillin, Pete Pihos, Roger Staubach

Cornell University, 46

Crisler, Fritz, 53, 59, 60. *See also* University of Michigan

Crowley, Jim, 77, 78. *See also* All-America Football Conference, University of Notre Dame

Culpepper, Daunte, 163. *See also* integration of professional football

Cunningham, Randall, 162, 163 *See also* integration of professional football, Philadelphia Eagles, University of Nevada Las Vegas

Dallas Texans, 121–126, *121, 124, 125,* 126, *129,* 131. *See also* Baltimore Colts, Art Donovan, Gino Marchetti, Giles Miller, National Football League

Davidson, Cotton, 134. *See also* Baltimore Colts

Deal, Russel, 39, *51, 52, 57. See also* Indiana University

Denver Broncos, 159, 160. *See also* American Football League, Marlin Briscoe, Joe Divito, Steve Tensi

Deranek, Dick, 41, *57. See also* Indiana University

Detroit Lions, 94, 102, 128. *See also* Mel Groomes, Bo McMillin, National Football League

Dickey, Eldridge, 159. *See also* American Football League, integration of professional football, Oakland Raiders, Tennessee State University

Dillon, Bobby, *125. See also* Green Bay Packers

Divito, Joe, 159. *See also* American Football League, Denver Broncos

Donovan, Art, 123. *See also* Dallas Texans

Dungy, Tony, ix, 158, 161, 163, 164. *See also* Indianapolis Colts, integration of professional football, University of Minnesota, National Football League, Super Bowl XLI

Eagleson, Preston, 36, 37. *See also* Indiana University

East Chicago Roosevelt High School, 10–13

Enke, Fred, 131. *See also* Baltimore Colts

Evans, Vince, 163. *See also* integration of professional football

Ewbank, Weeb, 133, 137. *See also* Baltimore Colts

Fisher, Gordon, *31. See also* Indiana University

Follis, Charles, 79. *See also* integration of professional football, Shelby Athletic Club

Fortman, Dan, 134. *See also* Chicago Bears

Friedlund, Arthur J., 110. *See also* All-America Football Conference

Garrett, Bill, 16, 86, 97, 99, 110. *See also* Big Ten, Indiana University

Gary, Indiana, 2–19, 20, 28, 137, 154, 156, 157. *See also* Charles Adkins, Lee Calhoun, Gary Roosevelt High School, Tom Harmon, Alex Karros, Willie Williams, Tony Zakm

Gary Roosevelt High School, 2, 6–19, 111. *See also* Gary, Indiana, Bo Mallard

Gator, Tony, 64. *See also* Army

Gill, Cordell, 144. *See also* Indiana University

Gilliam, Joe, Jr. ("Jefferson Street"), 160, 161. *See also* Terry Bradshaw, integration of professional football, Pittsburgh Steelers, Tennessee State University

Goldsberry, John, 21, 39, *51,* 52, 53, *57.* *See also* All-American, Big Ten (under all Big Ten), Indiana University

Grambling University, 160, 161

Great Depression, 4, 80, 81; New Deal, 93; Franklin Delano Roosevelt, 93

Green Bay Packers, *125,* 127 128. *See also* Charlie Brackins, Bobby Dillon, National Football League

Green, Charlie, 159. *See also* integration of professional football

Green, John, 68. *See also* Army, College Football Hall of Fame

Groomes, Mel, 37, 39, 41–46, *43,* 50, 76, 86, *89,* 102. *See also* Detroit Lions, Indiana University

Guglielmi, Ralph, 152. *See also* University of Notre Dame, Washington Redskins

Halas, George ("Papa Bear"), 38, 102, 117. *See also* Chicago Bears, University of Illinois, integration of professional football

Haley, Alex, 5

Harbison, Bob, *47. See also* Indiana University

Harmon, Tom, 157. *See also* Gary, Indiana, University of Michigan

Harrell, Paul, *31. See also* Indiana University

Harris, James ("Shack"), 160, 161. *See also* Buffalo Bills, Grambling University, integration of professional football

Harvard College, 25, 51. *See also* Centre College, Bo McMillin

Highbaugh, Larry, 145. *See also* Indiana University

Hillenbrand, Billy, 39, 40. *See also* All-American, Indiana University

Hoernschmeyer, Bob, 108. *See also* Chicago Hornets, Indiana University

Houston Oilers, 162. *See also* Warren Moon, National Football League

Howard, Sherman, 101, 102, 113, 115–117, 155. *See also* New York Yankees

Howard University, 66, 95, 141.

Huffman, Vern, 39, 40, 94. *See also* All-American, Big Ten (under MVP), Indiana University

Illinois, University of, 26, 43, 44, 100, 103, 112. *See also* George Halas, Buddy Young, Bob Zuppke

Indiana University, ix, 2, 14–16, 18–60, 70, 76, 83–100, 102, 104, 105, 108, 112, 115, *116,* 121, 130, *130,* 132, 138, 139, 142–144, 147–156, 160; Corso, Lee, and, 146, 147, 149, 150; Kinsey Report and, 85; Knight, Bob, and, 147–149; Old Oaken Bucket, 26, *27,* 40, 50, *50,* 52, 89, 144; Pont, John, and, 143–145, 149; Rose Bowl and, 144; segregation on the campus of, 21, 29–35, 56, 65, 66, 85–87, 100, 101; 1969 boycott and, 143, 144; Wildermuth, Ora, and, 16

Indianapolis Colts, ix, 158, 164. *See also* Baltimore Colts, Tony Dungy, National Football League, Super Bowl XLI

integration of professional football, 79–83, 158–164. *See also* American Professional Football Association, Jeff Blake, Charlie Brackins, Marlin Briscoe, Sol Butler, Chicago Black Hawks, Daunte Culpepper, Randall

A cartoon depicting George Taliaferro during the 1948 season, his last football season at Indiana University before going pro. *Courtesy George Taliaferro.*

Native Hoosier Dawn Knight received her B.S. in English from Indiana University and her M.A. in Journalism from Ball State University. She teaches English at Westfield High School in Westfield, Indiana. This is her first book.